THE
WORLD *M*YTHOLOGY
SERIES

Demons,
Gods & Holy Men
from
Indian
Myths and Legends

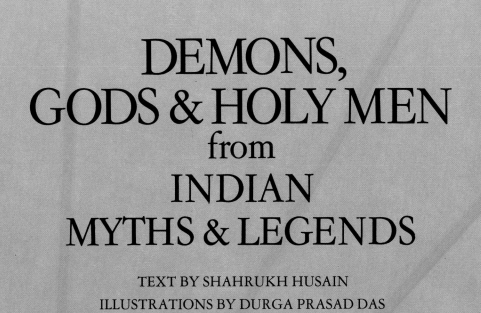

DEMONS, GODS & HOLY MEN
from
INDIAN MYTHS & LEGENDS

TEXT BY SHAHRUKH HUSAIN

ILLUSTRATIONS BY DURGA PRASAD DAS

PETER BEDRICK BOOKS

NEW YORK

Peter Bedrick Books
2112 Broadway
New York, NY 10023

Published by agreement with Eurobook Ltd, England

Library of Congress Cataloging-in-Publication Data
Shahrukh Husain.
    Demons, gods & holy men from Indian myths & legends / text by
Shahrukh Husain ; illustrations by Durga Prasad Das.
      p. cm. – (The World Mythology series)
    Includes index.
    Originally published: New York : Schocken Books, 1987.
    ISBN 0-87226-923-X
    1. Mythology, Hindu – Juvenile literature. 2. Mythology, Indic.-
-Juvenile literature. 3. Mythology, Hindu. 4. Mythology, Indic.
I. Das, Durga Prasad. II. Title. III. Title: Demons, gods, &
holy men from Indian myths & legends. IV. Series.
BL1111.32.E5S53 1995
294.5'13 – dc20   94-38057
                                                CIP

Printed in Italy by
Grafiche Editoriali Padane, Cremona
5 4 3 2 1 95 96 97 98 99

THE AUTHOR
Shahrukh Husain is a writer, lecturer and broadcaster. She
has a degree in South Asian Studies and has undertaken
further research on contemporary Urdu literature,
especially poetry, and South Asian music. Her interest in
mythology and folklore dates back to her childhood in
Pakistan and India where she had many opportunities to
listen to travelling storytellers and watch traditional theatre.

THE ARTIST
Durga Prasad Das lives and works in Orissa, India, where
he is Principal of the College of Art and Crafts. His
paintings have won numerous awards from organizations
such as the Academy of Fine Arts, Calcutta and the Andhra
Pradesh Council of Artists and are displayed in art
collections both in India and abroad.

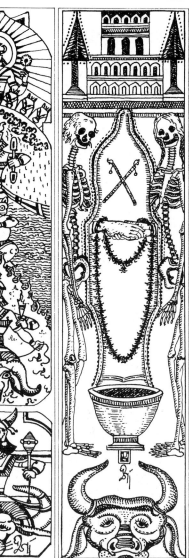

Contents

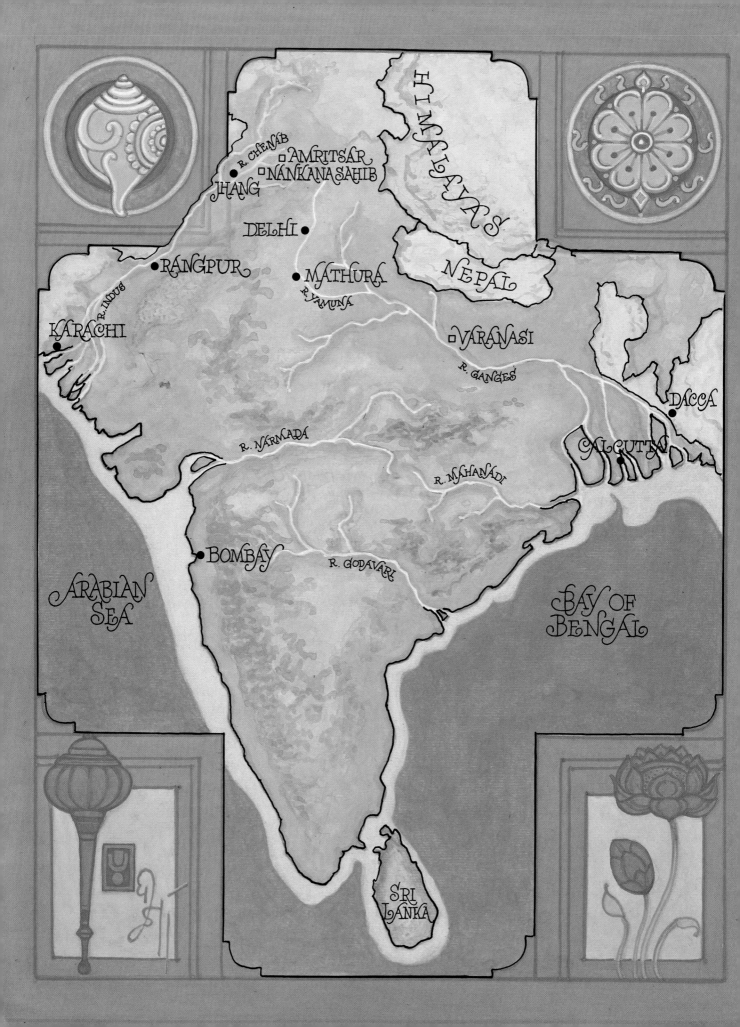

HIMALAYAS

R. CHENAB
AMRITSAR
□ NANKANA SAHIB
● JHANG

DELHI

NEPAL

● RANGPUR

R. INDUS

MATHURA
R. YAMUNA

□ VARANASI

R. GANGES

KARACHI

DACCA

CALCUTTA

R. NARMADA

R. MAHANADI

BOMBAY
R. GODAVARI

ARABIAN
SEA

BAY OF
BENGAL

SRI
LANKA

The world of the ancient Indians

The Himalayan mountains extend more than 1500 miles eastwards from Afghanistan to Bangladesh and separate the sub-continent of South Asia from the rest of the world. Since prehistoric times settlers and traders have travelled to and from India by mountain passes or by sea but for thousands of years its peoples remained largely isolated. This separation helped to create a way of life and system of thought which is markedly different from that of the West. The region is now divided into the independent countries of Afghanistan, Bangladesh, Bhutan, India, Nepal, Pakistan and Sri Lanka but their citizens share many beliefs and traditions.

Some Stone Age tools and weapons found in India date back to around 10,000 BC but the earliest prehistoric settlements that we know of were built in about 4000 BC in the valley of the River Indus in Pakistan and north-western India. By 3000 BC the Indus valley already had an organized system of government over an area greater in extent than the combined civilizations of Egypt and Mesopotamia which also existed at this time. Its ancient towns such as Harappa and Mohenjo Daro were well-planned with strong multi-storey houses built from baked brick and were superior in many ways to the ancient cities of Mesopotamia and Egypt.

Around 1000 BC tribes known as Aryans invaded India from Iran and Central Asia and brought with them a religion which later became known as Hinduism. It became the principal religion of South Asia and has had a profound effect on the social life of the people. One of the beliefs which the Aryans introduced into Indian society was that every man had specific jobs to perform in life. These fell roughly into four categories or castes. The two groups at the top of the hierarchy were the Brahmins and the Kshatriyas. It was the task of the Brahmins to learn, teach, perform religious sacrifices and act as mediators between the gods and men while it was the duty of the Kshatriyas to protect the people. The Kshatriyas were obliged to acquire the skills of war in order to fight battles and to study the arts of kingship in order to be just and wise rulers. The third group were the Vaishyas, who were traditionally farmers and businessmen. The function of the fourth group, the Sudras, was to wait on members of the other three classes or castes.

Outside this caste system were the Untouchables who had many occupations, such as carrying and cremating corpses, hunting, fishing, carpentry, sweeping and liquor-making. Some of the Untouchables were despised because their jobs were connected with death, whether of humans or other living creatures, others because they were menial. Whatever caste a person belonged to, it was the duty of all to perform their obligations to the best of their ability.

The Aryans also brought a belief in reincarnation or rebirth with them into India. It was thought that after people died, their souls would be rewarded or punished in the other world depending on how well they had behaved when alive. After a while, the soul would be reborn as a member of a higher caste if it had previously led a good life or into a lower caste if it had not. In all, a person would be born 82,000 times until finally if a person had reached the highest caste of Brahmin and lived a devout life in his final incarnation, he would receive eternal peace and release from the cycle of rebirth. Consequently, those living as members of lower castes had little to hope for in the foreseeable future.

However, in the sixth century BC two new religions known as Buddhism and Jainism arose, and these gave the lower members of society more hope. They preached that release was not reserved for the Brahmins alone and that members of the lower castes could escape rebirth if they performed certain pious acts. Many similar beliefs began to gain force in the Middle Ages.

The followers of all these religions wish to achieve eternal peace since they believe that the mortal world is a place of suffering and hardship and the only way to avoid pain is to escape the cycle of death and rebirth. This is also the ultimate goal of those holy men known as 'ascetics' who are common in India. Ascetics come from many different religions but all believe that the body is inferior to the soul and hampers its proper spiritual development. Accordingly, ascetics reduce temptation by controlling and conquering their bodily wants through prayer, fasting and meditation.

The idea of human rebirth or reincarnation or rebirth should not be confused with the idea that the gods, too, may be born on Earth in human form, as avatars. There are a countless number of gods in Hinduism and some of them returned to Earth again and again, but the gods came to Earth only when they chose to do so in order to help mortals whom they favoured. They did not have to go through the cycle of birth and death repeatedly.

Of all the gods Vishnu is said to have been born as an ordinary man the most often. This is because his purpose is to preserve the world from harm and so he sometimes causes a portion of himself to be born in human form in order to save the world from certain destruction. Buddhists believe that the spirit of the Buddha could also have rested eternally in Heaven after its very first birth. However, it was not content to have earned eternal peace for itself and wished to return continually to help others learn the true way.

The ancient mythology of India was essentially about rituals, morals and ethics and taught that there were two basic ways to earn religious merit. People could live an ordinary life and honour the gods by offering sacrifices and maintaining a high moral code. This would assure them a good life on Earth and after dying they would taste the pleasures of Paradise until they had to return to Earth once again. Alternatively they could become ascetics and give up the normal life of home and family to live a life of devotion and search for divine knowledge. Their self-denial in this world would ensure that they gained eternal peace after death and would never have to return.

The gods of Hindu mythology appear to be divided in the same way into 'spiritual' and 'worldly' beings. Early Indians often belonged to agricultural and fishing communities and relied on good weather for their livelihood. The early gods therefore, were cosmic personifications and could be friendly or malicious. Indra (Atmosphere), Agni (Fire) and Surya (Sun) were the most important of the friendly deities and Vritra (Drought), Vayu (Storm) and Yama (Death) were among those most feared. All of these early gods had the power to grant favours to their worshippers but were not concerned with people's souls.

Some time later when people began to think of life after death and the importance of the soul, there arose a triad of gods with a more spiritual function. They were Brahma (the creator), Vishnu (the preserver) and Shiv (the destroyer and re-creator). These deities look after the souls of mortals and the less important gods and it is through them that Hindus hope to gain divine knowledge and a place in the higher planes of the universe.

The universe of Hindu myths consists of three worlds: physical, heavenly and spiritual. A cosmic ocean of milk underlies everything and in it there are seven island continents of which the central and largest one is Jambu-dwip, the physical world. Jambu-dwip is protected by eight guardians, each with an elephant and each at a point of the compass. These are Indra (east), Agni (south-east), Yama (south), Surya (south-west), Varuna (west), Vayu (north-west), Kuvera (north) and Som (north-east). In the centre of this vast island and to the north of the Himalayas is a golden mountain named Meru which is flanked by four smaller mountains.

On top of Mount Meru is Brahmalok, the domain of Brahma the creator where souls go after attaining permanent release from the cycle of birth and death. This kingdom is surrounded by the celestial cities of the gods including Svarg which is ruled by Indra, chief of the devs or nature gods. There dwell the Sapta-rishi, the priests, known as Prajapatis, and minor nature gods—some of whom were once mortals. The Gandharvs, who are the heavenly musicians and the Apsarases, who are heavenly nymphs live in the foot-hills of Meru. In its valleys live rakshasas, the giants, goblins and devourers of human flesh who who try to gain superiority over the gods; asuras, evil spirits with supernatural powers who constantly disturb sacrifices; and other demons.

Between the Himalayas and the sea is India, the only country whose people experience suffering and therefore redemption. The other countries of the Hindu universe do not experience changes in time, and the people who live in them are always young and happy. Below India is the region of the dead. This consists partly of Hells of various grades of severity ruled over by the god Yama, and partly of the seven lands of the Nagas. The Nagas are serpent-gods with supernatural powers. Their supreme ruler is Shesh or Vasuki upon whom Vishnu the Preserver rests when from time to time he falls asleep in the cosmic ocean. While Vishnu sleeps the universe itself is periodically destroyed and reborn.

First, the whole world is submerged in the Cosmic Ocean and comes to an end. In these waters Brahma places a seed which grows into an egg. When it hatches, half its shell flies upwards to form the sky while the lower half forms the Earth. Brahma himself is the centre and creates the three worlds. One single day or night for Brahma is equal to an Earthly cycle lasting 4,320,000,000 years. There are in all, fourteen such phases of creation each headed by a Manu, a being who is simultaneously the teacher and father of that cycle of creation. Ours is the seventh phase and was led by the son of Surya the Sun, who is called Manu Vaivaswat. At the end of a hundred Brahma years, the three worlds will come to an end. After another hundred such years filled with chaos and disorder a new Brahma will arise to create a new universe.

India is the only country whose mythological culture has survived through the centuries and exists uninterrupted to this day. Many religions have been founded in India and others have been brought by immigrants such as the Zoroastrians who came in the fourteenth century AD and the Muslims who came as early as the seventh century AD as traders, settlers and missionaries.

The arrival of the Muslims eventually led to the creation of Pakistan and Bangladesh, which are separate Islamic countries. The Muslims contributed a great deal to the body of legend, folklore, music and language which is shared by the whole sub-continent. The stories in this book come from many parts of the sub-continent and include tales from the great Hindu epics and poems as well as legends of the saints, heroes and holy men from the past.

The old gods

The ancient Sanskrit text known as the *Rig-veda* is thought to have been composed as long ago as 1500 BC, and it contains the earliest description of the Hindu religion. It relates how a god presides over each of the three worlds of Hindu mythology: Indra (rain and dew) over the atmosphere, Surya (the Sun) over the sky, and Agni (fire) over Earth. Each of these elements was crucial to the survival of ancient agricultural communities and each god was worshipped and given offerings when his help was needed.

There were hundreds of other gods of different degrees of importance. Among the most ancient is Dyaus-Pitar, the heavenly father whose consort was Prithvi (Earth), the mother of all things. Other deities included their daughter Ushas (dawn) and Varuna the sea god. Just as gods of fine weather represented the forces of good, so evil gods were concerned with bad weather: the Maruts were storm gods and were servants of Indra. Vritra was the god of drought and famine and was Indra's enemy.

Indra is the son of Heaven and Earth and is the King of the Gods although he is not always the most powerful. He was born at a time when the drought demon Vritra had gained control of the atmosphere and prevented the rain clouds from dropping their rain on the parched Earth, which became shrunken and dry in the glaring, baking heat of the merciless sun. The people prayed in despair for a saviour who would destroy Vritra and bring the rains to Earth again, and Indra was born in answer to their prayer. Like many of the gods he had four strong arms which he waved vigorously about. The newly born god immediately arose, majestic and brave, leaving his twin brother Agni sleeping in his crib. (Agni, god of fire, could not help to end a drought. It was Indra, ruler of the atmosphere and protector of the harvest, who was most needed.) Indra reached into the atmosphere and grasped a thunderbolt for a spear and the rainbow for a bow. In his third hand he held his sword and the fourth he left free. Then he accepted from his worshippers cup after cup of the invigorating Soma juice which he so loved, gaining greater courage with each draught. His worshippers gazed at him with admiration.

Indra had the ability to change into anything he chose which was a remarkable asset in war. Armed with his various wonderful weapons and the effects of the Soma juice, Indra flew into the sky in search of Vritra. He found Vritra high in the cloud-built towers from which he controlled the rain clouds. Changing from form to form, Indra attacked him and at last after a long struggle, Vritra fell from his towers and disappeared in the clouds. However, this was not the end of Vritra, for he was 'drought' and lived in the atmosphere to be revived again by those who chose to use him.

Tvashtri was not a god but a Brahmin yet he was such a skilled craftsman that the gods asked him to build their heavenly cities for them. He carried a great axe and made many heavenly weapons for the gods including Indra's thunderbolts. He also modelled husbands for wives while they were still unborn. Tvashtri's pupils, the Ribhus, were assigned the task of building Indra's chariots and in time became so skilful that Indra rewarded them by changing them into gods. Tvashtri considered that he was the one who deserved to be honoured and he became so jealous that he tried to kill them but failed. Consumed by envy and resentment, he decided to destroy Indra and in order to do so created a Brahmin son called Trishiras (the three headed) or Vishvarup (one of many guises).

Indra heard that this three-headed Brahmin prayed and fasted continuously; he was gaining such power through his austere way of life that Indra feared that eventually Trishiras would be able to destroy him. One of his heads was always reading a holy book or praying while the others kept watch or slept, and so he gained in knowledge three times faster than an ordinary man. Indra decided to use his favourite method of distracting holy men from their prayers: he sent down celestial maidens who danced and sang and enticed Trishiras in every imaginable way, but they had no success. Indra was reluctant to kill a Brahmin but he knew now that he had had to kill Trishiras before he became too strong.

The god approached the spot where Trishiras prayed, and hurled his thunderbolt at him, severing all three of his heads. Then as he walked over to the Brahmin's corpse, he felt a strange magnetic power coming from the three pairs of eyes. He bent over to close them, but was so overcome with guilt that he sat down beneath a tree and began to pray for forgiveness. As he did so the heads turned into a francoline partridge, a sparrow and a common partridge and flew off. Indra stayed beneath the tree doing penance for many years until a divine voice told him he had been forgiven and could now return to his loving wife Indrani.

Tvashtri, however, was resentful at the failure of the plot and at his son's death and he revived Vritra the drought god in the form of a demon-giant who rampaged over the Earth destroying everything that he touched. Indra set out to bring the demon under control, and enlisted the help of many other gods but in spite of all their efforts the battle went badly for him. At one point Indra was caught between Vritra's teeth and held fast. Just in time, his twin brother Agni hurled an amulet of yawns at Vritra, causing him to grow drowsy and stretch his great jaws in a yawn so that Indra was able to escape. The gods then sought the advice of the great god Vishnu who told Indra to make peace with the demon and watch for a chance to kill him.

'When the time is right,' he promised Indra, 'I will help you.' Indra did as he was told and Vritra agreed to the truce under certain conditions.

'You will not kill me by night or by day, nor with a wet or dry weapon, nor with one made from wood, stone or metal,' he said and Indra agreed.

They became friends and stayed so for many years, but one day as they stood beside the seashore, Indra knew that the time had come to kill Vritra. It was late evening—twilight, which is neither day or night. Looking about him he saw the foam of the ocean—'Neither dry nor wet,' he thought cunningly, 'nor made from wood, stone or metal.' Indra bent down and began to hurl the foam at Vritra and by the power of Vishnu who infused the foam with his might, Vritra was smothered to death. Indra was so ashamed of his own deceit in killing a friend, however evil he may have been, that he disappeared for many years.

Since Indra was the god of the elements, his
disappearance cast the world into complete
chaos. The other gods searched everywhere for
him but were unable to find him. They decided
that they must choose another king for Indra's
kingdom of Svarg. They approached a king
named Nahush who although a mortal, was just
and wise. After some hesitation, Nahush agreed
to rule Svarg and was given Indra's wonderful
palace to live in. He had the freedom of his
garden, and even rode his elephant and sat in his
chariot. Gradually, Nahush grew arrogant. One
day he caught sight of Indra's wife, the
beautiful Indrani who had remained behind in
the palace. Nahush spoke to the gods.
'I am now king of Svarg and it is fitting that
Indrani should be my queen.'

The gods pleaded with Nahush to spare
Indrani since she still loved Indra deeply, and
when Nahush insisted, Indrani fled and took
refuge with Vrihaspati the teacher of the gods.
Nahush, who now in his arrogance treated the
gods as servants, sent the wind-gods after her,
demanding they bring Indrani before him.
'I will speak to Indrani,' said the teacher
Vrihaspati, 'but she has sought refuge here and I
will not compel her to leave.' Then he advised
Indrani to see Nahush and agree to marry him
if she could not find Indra within a few days.
Realizing this would buy her time, Indrani did
as he told her. Nahush agreed to her suggestion
and Indrani returned to Vrihaspati's house.

That night she prayed to Upashruti, goddess
of the night, to take her to her lord. The
goddess appeared and led Indrani over
mountains, through forests and beneath waters
until they arrived at a lake filled with lotuses.
'In that lotus,' she said, pointing to a large
flower in the middle of the lake, 'lives your
lord. I will take you to him.'

Indrani closed her eyes and Upashruti took
her beneath the surface of the lake to the stem
of the lotus which she split open with her mace.
Inside the stem, reduced to the size of a bee, sat
Indra. Indrani magically shrank herself until she
was as small as he was and entered the stem to
speak to him. Together they worked out a
strategy to defeat Nahush.

Next day Indrani sent a message to the king.

She agreed to be his wife on condition that he came to fetch her in a chariot drawn by the seven great sages known as the Sapta-rishi. Nahush accepted her condition at once and the seven great sages who could control Heaven and Earth at will, were yoked to his chariot. The sages began pulling the chariot to Indrani's home but although they had great magic powers they had only the strength of men and could only pull the chariot very slowly. This made King Nahush extremely impatient. He noticed that one of the sages was far smaller than the others and, concluding that the slow progress of the chariot must be his fault, prodded him sharply with his foot. Now this sage was Agastya, a well-known and very powerful man. He was so infuriated by the king's behaviour that he responded with the curse, 'May you become a serpent.'

As soon as he had spoken, Nahush was transformed into a snake and slithered away in shame to do penance. The glory of being the King of Heaven had been too great for a mere human to manage. Indra and Indrani's plan had succeeded and the god returned to Svarg and ruled happily from then on as lord of the firmament.

Agni: god of fire

Agni the god of fire is one of the best-known and loved of Hindu gods. He lives in all homes for it is he who warms them and cooks the food. He is present at Hindu wedding ceremonies because it is he who witnesses and blesses marriages, acting as a messenger to ask the other gods to come and do the same. He is a necessary part of all sacrifices for he purifies the offerings people cast into his flames before they are received by other gods. Although he is the son of Heaven and Earth, Agni is repeatedly born by the marriage of two pieces of dry wood, which, if rubbed together, produce a fire. He quickly devours these earthly parents with his flames and when he is blazing to his full height he begins to feed on the gifts of butter which are thrown to him by worshippers: then he calls to the other gods to come and share the offering.

Once Agni felt he had eaten too much of the rich food given to him by worshippers. Sick and exhausted from purifying the butter in his flames, he lost his strength and beauty. He needed to eat something more nourishing, something containing strength-giving minerals, and so he went to the Khandav forest which was ruled over by the Pandavs of Indraprastha. There he roamed, bedraggled and wild, trying to find a way to devour the forest, and satisfy his craving for food. At every step, he was foiled by his twin brother Indra, king of the gods, and protector of life on Earth, because Indra knew the destruction that Agni could cause. But Agni had set his heart on the Khandav forest and he wandered about in it until his tall body grew thinner than ever and his gold skin dulled. His blonde hair turned greasy and lustreless and his butter-smeared mouth began to gape with hunger and greed, revealing his glittering gold teeth which looked sharp and dangerous.

As he staggered about in exhaustion, he met a famous prince named Arjun accompanied by his uncle Krishna. Arjun belonged to the Pandav dynasty which owned the forest and Krishna was no ordinary mortal. In fact he was another incarnation of the supreme god Vishnu in human form.

'Feed me,' Agni rasped, 'I am a poor, hungry man.'

Arjun was full of pity at the sight of this wild and obviously starved man.

'What do you desire?' he asked.

'The Khandav forest,' replied Agni at once.

Arjun and Krishna exchanged glances dubiously. The Khandav forest was a large area of land and one they would not part with easily. Finally Krishna spoke.

'What of the people and animals in the forest?'

'There are no people,' replied Agni eagerly, 'and the animals will escape at the first sign of my feasting. Even the roots of the trees will survive for they are well beneath the soil and I only crave what is above the surface.'

'In that case, so be it,' said Krishna.

Agni looked dour. 'Indra will not let me,' he

scowled. 'But if you will agree to protect me from him, I will give you the weapons with which to do it.' So saying, he gave a magical bow to Arjun (who was famous for his superb archery) as well as two arrow-filled quivers which would never be empty. Finally he produced out of thin air a many-coloured chariot that shone like a rainbow, drawn by four fiery white horses and bearing a banner with a crest depicting an angry ape. In the chariot was Vishnu's famous weapon: his magic discus. Krishna smiled, 'We will see that you eat without interference.'

Agni heaved a great sigh of relief and as he breathed out, his nostrils blew out a thick, black smog. At that moment fire departed from all the three worlds of Heaven, Sky and Earth, leaving hearth, oven, sacrifice and ceremony. The world grew cold and dark, shaking and trembling in confusion, cold and fear. As the tongues of flame left their fireplaces they appeared by Agni's side and attached themselves to his body so that he was surrounded by fire and a fierce heat. Seven massive tongues of flame grew out of his own head, and his hair was ablaze.

Every time Agni breathed out, a scorching

wind appeared. Every time he breathed in, he sucked in trees, brush and scrub from the forest. Black clouds filled the sky as the fire raged through the forest. Agni stooped down and allowed his flames to flicker out into the undergrowth and devour all he could at ground level. Then he drew himself to his full height and threw his head back. His flames reached out over his head, feasting on the treetops. It was so hot that clouds of steam rose from the forest rivers to become rain clouds, and soon it was raining torrents of water. Yet they had no effect on the fire. Meanwhile, Prince Arjun showered the air with so many arrows that they formed a great curtain between Sky and Earth, preventing anyone trespassing and protecting the moon from the heat and smoke.

Agni continued eating the forest until at last Indra appeared on his magnificent white elephant, holding a thunderbolt in one hand. Beside him was Varuna the ocean god riding a fish and holding a noose ready to snare Agni. Close behind came Yama, god of death, mounted on a buffalo and bearing his fearsome mace; Kartikkeya, god of war on a peacock; Kuvera, god of wealth in a chariot; Surya the Sun wielding a dazzling and fiery dart and his sons the Ashwins bearing cups of poison. They formed a protective ring around Indra, who flung his thunderbolt towards Agni, but Krishna swiftly hurled his discus to intercept the thunderbolt which was shattered in a moment. The collision of the two mighty weapons caused an earthquake and Indra immediately bowed before Krishna, acknowledging defeat. The gods stood back and allowed Agni to continue his devastation. Soon Agni had completed his feast and stood before the gods, restored.

His dark eyes blazed vitality, his tongue was a shiny crimson and his skin glowed a deep molten gold. His hair was a mass of smoke. Agni was clothed in velvety black and bore in one hand a standard formed of smoke with a crest of fire while in another hand he held a flaming javelin. Bowing deeply, he thanked Krishna and Arjun for their support. Then Agni called the ram on which he often rode and summoned his chariot which had the seven

winds for its wheels and was drawn by six red horses. He lifted his ram into the chariot beside him and flew off to guard again the south-east quarter of the universe which was under his protection. After that, fire came back into the lives of the people with a new vigour and vitality.

Surya and Sanjna

Surya the great Sun god was one of the three chief gods of ancient Hinduism. He was the source of all light and warmth and each night he rode across the sky in a flaming chariot drawn by a seven-headed horse. He was himself radiant and fiery although dwarfish in stature with red eyes and a body which glimmered and glinted like burnished copper.

Once during a visit to the celestial craftsman Vishvakarma, Surya fell in love with his daughter Sanjna. She also grew to love him in spite of her father's repeated warnings. 'The heat of Surya in his full glory or rage is unbearable. Even the gods cannot stand it,' he warned. But Sanjna was determined to marry Surya, and at last her father gave his consent to the marriage.

For some years after their marriage they lived happily and Sanjna gave birth to a son, Manu Vaivaswat, and twins, Yama and Yamini. Then one day at noon, Sanjna ventured near her husband who glowed and throbbed in the full passion of his zenith. He tried to kiss her, but she backed away, feeling the intensity of his extreme heat and afraid that his touch would burn her to ashes. The Sun god was offended. 'So, you refuse to be near me although you swore everlasting devotion! I curse you through your children. Your eldest son, Manu Vaivaswat, will be banished from heaven. At the beginning of the next age he will live on Earth as the next father of mankind. There he will remain alone for years. Your son Yama will be king of the underworld, lonely and despised by all, condemned to bring misery to mankind—he will be the god of death. Your daughter Yamini will be fickle like you and will live in the form of a wayward river. Their suffering will cause

because she consistently favoured her own children, and raised his foot to kick her. Chaya cursed him so that his foot became afflicted with sores which oozed worms. Stunned by Chaya's vengeful behaviour, Surya finally realized she was not his real wife Sanjna.

He gave Yama a cockerel to pick out the worms on his leg, and having wrung the truth from Chaya set out to find his real wife. It was not long before Surya found Sanjna (who was still living as a mare) and he began to court her in the form of a white horse, showing how kind and gentle he could be. During their courtship they had three sons: the twin Ashwins who draw the sun chariot across the sky at dawn, and Revanta, king of the Guhyakas, the invisible beings who guard the treasures of Kuvera, god of wealth. Only then did Surya tell his wife who he was.
'I have known all along,' she replied, 'but I fear you as the Sun god and cannot come back.'

Downcast, Surya went to his father-in-law and asked him if he had a solution.
'Enter my lathe,' Vishvakarma said, 'and let me trim an eighth of your radiance away. Then Sanjna will have nothing to fear.'

Surya unhesitatingly did as he suggested and soon one eighth of each of the rays of his body was removed. Only his feet stayed as brilliant as ever. Then Surya went to Sanjna and explained what he had done. She was so moved by his sacrifice that she returned with him to their home. There they lived in harmony ever after, with the penitent Chaya, the shadow, as their handmaid.

Yama: god of death

Yama, god of death, ruled over Yamapur in the underworld from his enormous, dark palace called Kalichi. Several times a day he seated himself on his throne of judgement to hear the testimony of the newly dead souls who were brought to him by his messengers, the Yama-dutas. His councillor read out the accounts of the dead from a massive register, and Yama decided on the fate of the soul. If it belonged to someone who was good, it would

you far greater pain than any I could inflict directly upon your body.'

When Sanjna heard her husband's terrible words she began to appreciate the extent of his ferocity. She fled to a forest and looking deep into the waters brought her reflection to life. She named it Chaya, which means reflection or shadow.
'You are shadow,' Sanjna told her, 'and you can live with the heat and ferocity of the Sun. Be kind to my children and do not give away my secret.' Saying this she turned herself into a mare so that Surya would not trace her, and devoted her life to prayer.

For some years Chaya lived in peace with Sanjna's husband and children and bore him two sons, Sani the planet Saturn, and Manu Savarni, the father of mankind in another age as well as a daughter Tapti, a river. The other children were unaware that Chaya was not their mother and one day Yama became furious

go to the heavens of Pitris or Svarg where it would enjoy many years of pleasure and comfort before returning to the mortal world in another form. If it had been in the body of someone who was evil then it would be assigned to one of twenty-one hells according to the magnitude of its sins.

Yama was a just ruler but very grim and serious. His skin was green and his garments were red. In one hand was an enormous and fearsome mace and in the other a noose with which he secured his victims. His mount was a large buffalo. He had other messengers apart from the Yama-dutas: two insatiable dogs with four eyes each and enormous, flaring nostrils that belched smoke. They guarded the road to Yamapur but often wandered about among the people of the world in order to carry them off to their master when the end of their days arrived. Occasionally Yama sent a bird of doom to announce a person's death.

Yama was not a great favourite among the other gods. They avoided him because he was associated with the dead and therefore brought fear and sorrow to those still living. The gods therefore left him very much alone. To make up for his lack of company, Yama married many wives. Once he fell in love with a Brahmin's daughter named Vijaya. At first Vijaya was afraid of this strange god but soon she realized he was just and good, and was the judge of the dead because of a curse laid on him by his father the Sun god Surya.

Vijaya felt affection and sympathy for Yama and married him in spite of her father's protests. Shortly after she came to live with Yama in Kalichi, he said to her, 'You have the freedom of all of my kingdom except the southern quarter.' Vijaya explored the palace and the whole of her husband's domain until only the southern quarter was left. At first she heeded Yama's words and did not go there but the more she thought about it, the more curious she became.

'He must have a secret wife hidden there,' she thought suspiciously. 'One he loves more than the others and keeps separate so that she can be treated more lavishly.'

When she ventured near the forbidden area, she felt a great warmth radiating from it and saw an eerie glow. Occasionally she heard disturbing noises, but Vijaya did not know what they were. Although she was becoming frightened, Vijaya was a brave woman and was determined to investigate the place once and for all. Passing through a gateway of flame, she found herself in Hell. Horrified, she watched the tormented souls howling, shrieking and lamenting. Suddenly she heard her name and turned around to see who was calling her. To her extreme distress, Vijaya saw her dead mother suffering hideous punishments. In anguish she hurried back to Yama and begged him to release her mother.

'It is not possible,' replied Yama, but Vijaya persisted. At last Yama explained that if someone could be found on Earth to perform a particularly arduous sacrifice and transfer its merit to the dead woman, she would be released from the fires of Hell. Vijaya finally succeeded in finding such a person and Yama's mother-in-law obtained release.

Yama once fell in love with another mortal woman. He disguised himself as a man and won her hand, but it was not long before he discovered that the wife he had chosen was shrewish and querulous. She became even worse when she bore him a son named Yama-Kumar. Yama frequently disagreed with his mortal wife about the upbringing of the boy, but she argued so violently with him that in the end he agreed to whatever she said. Finally Yama was unable to bear her bad temper any more and returned to his kingdom. From there he kept an eye on his son who grew up under the wife's care quite incapable of looking after himself. One night Yama appeared to him and promised him the gift of healing if he would work very hard and learn about medicinal herbs and plants. This the boy did and after a year became a qualified doctor.

'I am proud of you, my son.' Yama told him. 'Now every time you approach a sick bed you will see me there. If the patient is curable I will nod: if not I will shake my head from side to side. When that happens, you must refuse to treat the patient.'

The boy agreed gratefully and soon became

widely known for his excellent diagnosis and treatment. Some years later a princess became very ill. Doctors came from far and near to cure her but they were all unsuccessful. The princess grew weaker and weaker and finally Yama-Kumar was called.

As he approached the bed, he saw his father, mace and noose in hand, looking ferociously down at the fragile young woman. When Yama-Kumar looked at him, Yama shook his head from side to side signalling that this girl was to die. For the first time, the healer chose to argue with his father.

'The girl is young and beautiful,' he said. 'Can you not let her remain with her family for a few more years?'

'Three days,' growled Yama, 'I shall give her three days more because you are my son and have pleased me. You would do well to speak to her parents and warn them that she has only a short time to live.'

Thanking his father, Yama turned to the king and queen who had been entirely unaware of the god's presence and instructions.

'Your majesties,' said the healer, 'your daughter is very ill. I think she has three days of life left.

However if she outlives these, she will live to a ripe old age.' Saying this he sat down beside her and began to nurse her.

When the three days were over Yama arrived at the princess's bedside ready to bear her away, but his son spoke first.

'Father,' he said slyly, 'if you attempt to take this girl away now or ever again before she has reached the age of a hundred years, then I will tell my mother who you are and how to reach you.'

Yama turned deathly pale at the mention of his wife's name and began to shiver. When he had recovered from his shock, he turned to his son with some amusement.

'You have reasoned well, my son,' he confessed, 'and as a reward I give you the life of the princess.'

As soon as Yama had left, the colour began miraculously to return to the princess's cheeks and all the healer's treatment began to take effect at once. After a week had passed, he announced to her family that she was cured. So happy were the king and queen that they married the young man to their daughter and the couple lived happily to a ripe old age.

The great goddesses

Female deities or shaktis were always recognized as the wives and helpers of the male gods, but it was only in the Middle Ages that they began to be worshipped in their own right. People had always believed that much of the power of the male gods came from their wives and that without their help the gods did not have their maximum creative powers. Gradually through the centuries many of the powers of the male gods were transferred to their wives who of course still had their own special qualities. Eventually the goddesses were considered to be almost more powerful than their husbands, and a religious sect called the Shaktas came into being whose main objects of worship were the goddesses Shakti (the Universal Mother), Savitri (Wisdom and Learning) and Lakshmi or Shri (Good Fortune). The goddesses are ideal objects of worship. Having the hearts of women, they are more accessible and sympathetic to the people and in addition to their own great powers they can often persuade their husbands to help as well.

Shakti is the mother goddess and has been worshipped in many forms: Devi, Parvati, Mahamaya, Durga and Jagad-janini are only some of her other names. She represents the wisdom of the universe and so when the gods decided that the great god Shiv needed a wife to help him, she was the obvious choice. Shiv is the destroyer and restorer of the universe, but he needed a wife to help him in his tasks. The gods persuaded the mother goddess to be reborn as Sati, the daughter of Daksha who had created mankind. Sati fasted and prayed from an early age, aware that she would have to prove her spiritual worth before Shiv would accept her for his wife. One day, after she had performed a particularly long fast, a man with his face hidden in his cloak came and criticized her for her choice of husband.

'Shiv is a disreputable fellow,' he said. 'He dresses in rags, haunts cremation grounds and cemeteries and keeps company with imps, goblins and other evil spirits. No-one knows who his parents are. You are the daughter of the creator of mankind. Why not choose a better husband?'

Sati replied simply that she believed all Shiv's actions had a deep-rooted universal significance. Therefore he was above criticism. Hearing this, the man dropped his cloak and revealed himself to be Shiv. 'You have pleased me, daughter of Daksha,' he stated. 'We will be married.' Shiv and Sati were married with great ritual and ceremony and went to live in Kailash, Shiv's home, where they spent many ages happily engrossed in each other and in their task of maintaining the universe.

Daksha, however, had always disliked Shiv and continually insulted him. Finally Sati could not tolerate his behaviour a moment longer. She threw herself on a sacrificial fire with a vow that she would return only when she was born to a father whom she could respect. Shiv reconstructed Sati's body from the ashes and held it in his arms.

'You are my energy, Sati,' he lamented. 'Without you I am little more than a corpse. As your husband and your lord, I ask you to return to me.'

The mother goddess, however, had returned to her original form and had no intention of being born again until she found a suitable father. Shiv smeared his body with Sati's ashes and, flinging a chain of her bones and relics around his neck, was left to wander around in distress.

Without Shiv and Sati's guidance, the universe began to fall into disarray until one day the mother goddess reappeared to Shiv. She was sitting on a cloud, her presence was glowing and luminous, and she was covered with beautiful jewels and flowers.

'I have been born again, my lord,' she told Shiv, 'and I shall soon be reunited with you. In reality, I have never been away from you and never shall.' Shiv felt a deep sense of relief when he heard this and began to concentrate again on bringing harmony to the world.

This time Shakti chose for her parents the noble chief of mountains, Hemavat, and his beautiful wife Mena, daughter of Mount Meru. The mother goddess took a new name each time she was reborn and this time she was known as Parvati. Soon after her birth a celestial voice urged her to begin fasting and praying to win the attention of Shiv, but Parvati was confident that he would come to her of his own accord.

She was both young and beautiful and she knew well how long the great god had mourned for her. However, Shiv had now returned to his task of maintaining the world, and this involved deep concentration which could only be broken by the power of the most intense prayer. He did not notice Parvati at all and even when she realized this and began to do penance she could not succeed in distracting Shiv.

The other gods realized that their assistance was needed, and the one who could best help was Kamadev the god of love. Kamadev rode on his parrot to Shiv's home, taking with him his wife Reva, the embodiment of passion. Together, they waited for the right moment to act. Soon Parvati approached. She was dressed in tree bark, her hair uncombed, her body smeared with ashes and she was calling to Shiv in despair. Shiv was momentarily distracted by the power of Parvati's prayers and at that instant Kamadev aimed his bow of sugar-cane, tautened its string formed by a line of bees and let loose an arrow tipped with a love-flower. The love-arrow found its mark and Shiv's love for his wife was reawakened.

Shiv was reunited with Parvati and the gods joined in their triumphal wedding procession. Indeed, the creatures of the heavenly worlds showered so many flowers on them that soon the couple were walking knee-deep in fragrant blooms. Parvati has never again been separated from Shiv and they spend their time happily together in their home on Kailash guiding the universe.

Durga and Kali

Although Parvati is normally as loving and kind as a mother goddess should be, her husband is Shiv who is lord of demons, goblins and other evil spirits, and like him she has a dark side to her character. One of the incarnations in which she is worshipped is Durga the ferocious warrior goddess. Durga is beautiful and serene, and rides into battle seated upon a lion. She has ten arms, each of which holds a weapon borrowed from the gods and her sole desire is to destroy demons.

In another of her incarnations she is Kali, who is usually shown with a black complexion and a red tongue. Kali has four hands: she holds a sword in the first and a giant's head in the second, and waves to her worshippers with the other two. For adornment, Kali wears a necklace of skulls; two dead bodies form her earrings while her skirt is made from the hands of dead evil-doers.

The most famous victory of Durga and Kali was over the giants Sumbha and Nisumbha whose armies were once powerful enough to defeat the gods themselves. The gods begged Shiv to protect them from the giants, but the giants were Shiv's worshippers and he refused to help although he did suggest that they approach Parvati instead.

The unhappy gods prayed to the mother goddess and her heart began to soften. Eventually she appeared to them in a radiant beam of light and promised to destroy the giants by turning herself into Durga.

As Durga the warrior goddess she rode on her lion to the lair of the giants at the top of the Himalayan mountains and challenged them to battle. A great army of giants fought her yet she killed and then devoured them as easily as if they were dried fruit. The giants Sumbha and Nisumbha had been watching at a safe distance but now they marched against her with a second army led by the giant commander Raktavij. The gods quaked in fear of the terrors to come but the goddesses were not afraid and they descended to Earth to help Durga, who attacked Raktavij fiercely with her ten deadly weapons. The giant was badly wounded, but a thousand giants as strong as he sprang from every drop of his blood which spilled onto the ground; eventually Durga was near to defeat.

In a desperate bid for victory she split herself in two. Part of her became the four-handed Kali, who drank the drops of the giant's blood before they touched the ground. Soon Raktavij was dead and the other goddesses killed the remaining giant soldiers. Finally Durga turned upon Sumbha and Nisumbha. After a ferocious battle she killed them too, and the goddesses filled the skies with their praise of Durga—the celestial heroine who had saved them all.

Lakshmi: goddess of love, luck and wealth

Lakshmi is perhaps the most popular of the goddesses since she is regarded as being especially close to the people, caring for everyone and unconcerned with their background or even their actions. She is like a woman who is perfect in many ways but is easily enticed by flattery and worship. When she is won over by her worshippers, she will grant them gifts of love, wealth and good fortune—which are after all the most desirable things in the world. But although she can be easily attracted, Lakshmi can also easily be tempted away by another devotee who might call a little louder or with greater endearments than the first one. When she leaves, her gifts often (though not always) go with her. Because of her faithlessness, she became known as Chanchal, 'the Fickle One'.

During the festival of Divali in October or November, Lakshmi roams the Earth in search of a place to spend the night and bestow her gifts. All over India hundreds of little oil lamps are lighted and placed around houses and roof-tops and even floated in ponds and streams to attract her to them. The whole of India is like

a fairyland, glittering and twinkling in devotion to this lovable goddess who never stays with anyone for long but is an eternal wanderer.

At the beginning of creation, when the powers of the gods were beginning to wane because a curse had been put on them by a sorcerer, they went to see the supreme god Vishnu. He advised them to churn the celestial ocean to obtain a life-giving draught of nectar. As they did so, the waves began to ripple with excitement, and floating on top of them was a lotus flower. From this stepped the goddess Lakshmi. When her beauty was revealed, even the heavens sang her praises and the heavenly dancers performed for her alone. All the world's streams and rivers flowed towards her and their waves beckoned to the heavenly elephants to suck up the pure waters in their trunks and bathe the exquisite goddess in them. When she had completed her bath, Lakshmi dressed herself in jewels and garments that were beautiful beyond description. Then the ocean gave her its own gift—a garland of fragrant and never fading blooms.

Lakshmi was young and beautiful, with skin the colour of gold with a sheen of pearls on it. Her large, luminous eyes were the shape of lotuses. Her black hair rolled down in waves to her knees. She wore so many exquisite jewels that she was like a vision of flashing, glowing lights as she stepped from the ocean's foam and walking over to Vishnu, she embraced him tenderly, making the watching gods and demons sick with jealousy and longing.

Lakshmi was born solely to be Vishnu's wife, amd although she was much desired by other gods, she remained faithful to her husband Vishnu and was reborn many times to accompany his incarnations—and each time a great love story was created. When Vishnu was born as the dwarf Vaman, she was born as Kamla; when he was Parasu-Ram, she was his wife Dharini; when he was Ram, she was Sita, and when he was Krishna she was Rukmini. In short, whenever Vishnu was born as a man, Lakshmi appeared as his human wife. When he was a god, she was a goddess. Vishnu is the male in everything and Lakshmi the universal female.

Sarasvati: goddess of learning

The River Sarasvati in northern India is the earthly embodiment of Sarasvati, the goddess of learning, who invented the Sanskrit language and the Devanagri script in which Sanskrit, Hindi and other Indian languages are written. She is also the patroness of arts, sciences and speech. As the river, Sarasvati presides over religious festivals and grants the Earth and its people fertility, strength and wisdom.

Sarasvati is eternally young, tall, and fair-skinned and has four arms. She sits elegantly on a lotus flower, playing a string instrument known as the vina which some say she invented herself. At other times she is portrayed standing by the side of her husband, presenting him with a lotus with one right hand. In her other right hand she holds a book of palm leaves, because she loves learning. In her two left hands she holds a small drum and a rosary of pearls.

Sarasvati is the wife of the Supreme Spirit Brahma and lives with him in Brahmalok where she is his true equal. It is said that Brahma grew his extra heads so that he could gaze at her wherever she was, so much did he love her, but their marriage was not always peaceful. One day Brahma was preparing an important religious sacrifice and sent a messenger to fetch Sarasvati, because she was late.

'I am not dressed,' replied Sarasvati, 'and I have several matters to see to before I can participate in Brahma's sacrifice. I shall attend the gathering in due course with Lakshmi, Parvati and Indrani, the wives of the other gods.'

The messenger returned to Brahma and reported what she had said. The god was infuriated by his wife's arrogance, especially since the proper time for the sacrifice was coming to an end. He turned to Indra.

'Go Indra,' Brahma said, 'and find a substitute for Sarasvati for I cannot make the sacrifice without a wife beside me.'

Accordingly, Indra set off and seeing a very beautiful and pious milkmaid called Gayatri, told her she was needed as a wife for Brahma and carried her off to Brahmalok. There she was dressed in glorious robes, decorated with

wonderful gems and seated in the bridal pulpit with the full approval of all the other gods.

The marriage ceremony was drawing to a close when Sarasvati arrived with Lakshmi, Parvati and Indrani in a carriage drawn by a heavenly swan. As the four goddesses stepped down from their carriage, Sarasvati was amazed to see that Brahma had married a second wife, and she was so infuriated that she reprimanded her husband publicly.

'Can it be true that you, Brahma, father of the gods and sages, could take a second wife while your first one still lives? And that in the presence of all these gods and holy men?'

Shame-facedly, Brahma explained that he had married Gayatri only because he had needed a wife for the sacrifice, and Sarasvati herself had refused to appear.

'Forgive me for this act Sarasvati, and you will never find me guilty of any offence again.'

But the goddess was not appeased.

'I am the possessor of many powers, achieved through learning and concentration. Now I use them to curse you and your companions in this act. You, Brahma the Supreme Spirit, will never be worshipped in any sacred place or temple except for once a year. You, Indra, King of the Gods, will be defeated and chained by your enemies and your kingdom Svarg will be occupied by them.'

Then she turned to Vishnu. 'You, Vishnu, Supreme Deity though you are, will be born ten times amongst men. In one such life, your wife will be ravished and you will suffer the anguish of being separated from her. In another incarnation you will be condemned to wander for years as a humble cowherd. You, Shiv, Supreme Creator, will never have any children of your own.'

Pronouncing these curses, Sarasvati swept from the assembly taking Lakshmi, Parvati and Indrani with her. After they had gone a short distance the other goddesses said that they wished to return to their husbands. Still angry, Sarasvati turned on them in her fury.

'Go then,' she screamed, 'but take these curses with you. Lakshmi, goddess of good fortune, you will wander forever, becoming known as fickle and as one who favours the evil and the avaricious rather than the good and truly needy. You Indrani will suffer the amorous advances of King Nahush, who will become king of Svarg while your husband lies suffering elsewhere.'

She then turned furiously on Parvati the Mother Goddess, but since she did not have the power to curse her, she addressed them all together.

'May you all become sterile so that no child is born to any one of you.' And she stormed away.

When they returned to the assembly, the goddesses found their husbands and their guests as deeply perplexed as they were. Everyone had forgotten about the pure and sinless milkmaid Gayatri who now spoke for the first time.

'I am no match for the great Sarasvati,' she said humbly. 'What she has pronounced must come to pass. But I have some magic power and can modify her curses to bring as little suffering as possible to you. Though you will be worshipped in a temple only once a year Lord Brahma, your worshippers will still be absorbed into you after death and you will be recognized as the Supreme Spirit. You, Lord Indra, after suffering the indignities Sarasvati has wished upon you, will be saved by your own wife and return to rule forever in Svarg. Lord Vishnu's wife will be kidnapped from him in his sixth incarnation, but she will return to him pure and chaste. And in all other incarnations she will be born as his consort and they will be inseparable. Each birth of Vishnu will be for the good of mankind and the destruction of evil. Though Lord Shiv will be infertile, he will be worshipped widely as the symbol of fertility. In addition, he will be praised all over India and all people will wish to be like him.'

She paused for a moment, her eyes resting on the anxious faces of the goddesses. 'You will not bear children as mortal women do, but you will not feel the lack of them, for your homes and hearts will be filled in many other ways.'

So it was that the destinies of all the major gods and goddesses were influenced by Sarasvati. In due course she forgave Brahma and returned to live with him in peace but it is in the world of people that she mainly lived and there she is still worshipped as the goddess of knowledge and wisdom.

Holy men of India

According to Hindu tradition, when Brahma the supreme spirit decided to put people on the Earth, he created seven 'rishis' or holy men from his thought waves. They are still visible in the constellation known as Ursa Major or the Great Bear while their wives glitter nearby in the constellation of the Pleiades. The rishis created seven 'manus' or saviours in seven ages of the world and from them everything living has sprung.

Hindu mythology is full of stories of these holy men, and there are also many myths, legends and folk tales about the founders and preachers of later religions which began or which have flourished in India. One such religion is Jainism, which began in India in the sixth century BC. Jains believe that there are countless souls who live in different parts of the universe depending upon their degree of merit. Stones, plants, insects and animals as well as people are all the temporary homes of souls and for this reason the Jains have great respect for all forms of life. Jainism was founded by a man named Vardhamana.

Vardhamana, later known as Jina (the conqueror) was born around 599 BC in a district called Besarh in north-eastern India. Many legends are now told about him, but he is definitely a historical figure. When he was born, people were divided into different castes with the Brahmins (holy men) and Kshatriyas (noble warriors) at the highest level of society; anyone who broke the laws of the caste system was harshly punished. People had to live in certain parts of the towns and cities, according to what caste they belonged to—in fact the quarters were so strictly defined that they were almost self-sufficient villages.

Vardhama was born into the affluent Kshatriya area of the city of Kundigram in Besarh. The area was ruled by a parliament made up of the chiefs of all the local Kshatriya clans with a king at their head. The king's daughter was Trishali, who was married to a chief named Siddharta.

One night she dreamed of a luminous white elephant: this magical creature appeared to all mothers due to bear a special person called a Trithankara—one who guides people across the troubled seas of life. The elephant was followed by a series of images which included a

33

white bull, the goddess Sri indicating the child's happiness and the red sun symbolizing the child's acquisition of perfect knowledge. When Trishali told her husband of her dreams, Siddharta summoned the best interpreters of dreams who explained that Trishali was to bear the perfect child who would bring the light of knowledge to the world forever.

Long before Trishali's dreams, the god Indra had discovered that a holy teacher was to be born on Earth. His mother was to be the wife of a poor, local Brahmin but Indra, unwilling to allow such a baby to be born into poverty, transferred the unborn child to Trishali's womb. The fortunes of Trishali and Siddharta improved greatly from the moment that she conceived, so that when the boy was born they called him Vardhamana, which means 'increase'.

Even as a child, the boy showed remarkable knowledge, physical prowess and fearlessness. Once he was playing with friends in a large park when a rogue elephant thundered in. Everybody scattered out of sight except for Vardhamana who approached the crazed beast gently and calmed it down; he then gripped the elephant's trunk and bravely climbed onto its back. On another occasion he had climbed a tree when a minor Hindu god lifted him onto his shoulders and flew into the air to frighten him. Fearlessly, the child gripped the god's hair in one fist while he struck him with the other so hard that the god cried out in pain and hastily replaced the child in the tree. The other gods were amused by the youngster's victory and named him Mahavira which means 'the brave conqueror.'

Vardhamana soon knew that he wished to lead the lonely life of an ascetic, but he did not want to hurt his parents who would, he knew, be upset by his decision so he decided to live normally during their lifetime. He married and had a daughter but when he was twenty-nine his parents died and Vardhamana told his older brother of his wishes. Since arguments often occurred in ruling families over the rights of inheritance, his brother asked him to wait for another year to prevent anyone thinking that they had quarrelled. Accordingly, a year later (about 570 BC) Vardhamana prepared to take

religious vows and become a monk.

The prince fasted for two and a half days, refusing even water. Then he gave away all his possessions and left for his initiation ceremony. Vardhamana had decided to take his vows under an ashoka tree in a large public garden near Kundigram. The gods themselves were to join in his initiation ceremony, and he wore a magnificent robe given to him by Indra. As he left his house to go to the gardens, a Brahmin who had been out of the town when Vardhamana was distributing his possessions hurried up to him and demanded his share. Vardhamana was distressed that he no longer had anything to give to him so he tore his magnificent robe in half and gave him part of that. Then he continued on his way.

When he reached the ashoka tree, he mounted the five-tiered throne which had been placed there facing east in preparation for the ceremony and gave the last of his clothes to the onlookers. Then, instead of shaving the hair from his head as was customary among ascetics, he pulled it out by the roots to show that he had no regard for his body. Jain monks follow his example to this day. Seeing this gesture, Indra fell to his feet to retrieve the hair and carry it off to safety.

Now began Vardhamana's long years of penance and prayer as he searched for enlightenment about the right way to live. He wandered through forests and villages in his quest but in spite of his holy way of life, supreme knowledge continued to elude him. During this time he succeeded in conquering physical sensations completely. Once as he sat praying by the roadside, some crude herdsmen decided to play a trick on him. They lit a fire between his feet and when he did not seem to notice its heat, they knocked nails into his ears. Even that did not disturb him.

By now Vardhamana had long since lost his clothes and since he had no physical or emotional need of them, he did not think of replacing them: even to this day, there is a sect of Jain priests in southern India who do not wear clothes. So, naked, Vardhamana continued to travel. The only time that he stayed in one place was during the rainy season when he rested under one roof for four months to avoid stepping on any new plants that had grown in the rain.

After twelve long years of searching, Vardhamana sat down to pray one day beneath a tree in a village called Samak. While praying there, he finally received enlightenment, and its message was for everyone no matter where or when they lived. He was now Jina, Conqueror of Truth. Soon afterwards he began teaching what he had learned. His message was simple: birth and caste do not matter. Instead it is important to overcome material desires in order to be able to escape from the Terrible Ones—Birth and Death—who relentlessly pursue the soul. Everything has a right to live, and he forbade the killing of any living thing, so much so that he did not even approve of eating roots.

Vardhamana's first followers were kings and noblemen who were delighted that one of them had challenged the power of the priestly Brahmins. He preached for forty-one years and travelled, it is said, with 14,000 disciples, preaching to vast audiences.

When Vardhamana was seventy-two (in 527 BC) he visited Papa in Patna (now a village called Pavapuri and still very important to the Jains). An enormous assembly had gathered to hear him and he sat on a throne of diamonds that had been built for him by the kings among his followers. Here Vardhamana delivered fifty-five lectures which lasted for six days and nights. Even the gods came to listen, and the hall shone with the fabulous light of their presence. When the morning of the seventh day came the great teacher knew he was to die. He began to meditate and passed quietly to the other world.

When his disciples looked again at the throne, they saw that nothing was left except his nails. They carefully took these and the hair that Indra had preserved, and cremated them with every ritual. Then the kings ordered hundreds of small lamps to be lit to replace in some small measure the light of Vardhamana's great knowledge. Some say that this is the origin of Divali, the festival of lights, which is celebrated by Jains and Hindus alike.

Siddharta—the Buddha

Buddhism is one of the world's great religions and like Jainism it began in northern India in the sixth century BC. Siddharta, its teacher, preached that all men are equal and that even the lowliest can escape the constant cycle of rebirth if they are good and generous. He preached that most of life's unhappiness is caused by people's desire for all kinds of trivial things. To get rid of the unhappiness you must free yourself from these desires by following a system of meditation and disciplined conduct. Siddharta became known as the Buddha, and his followers believe that his spirit was one that had achieved release from the endless cycle of reincarnation but chose to return to Earth as a man to show humanity the way to salvation. This is the story of his rebirth.

The spirit of the Buddha stirred in heaven. It was time for him to return to Earth after the short period of rest he allowed himself between his lives on Earth where, again and again, he returned to attain enlightenment and teach it to the world. This time he told his attendants that he had chosen as his mother Queen Mahamaya. She was the wife of King Sudhodhan who ruled Kapilavastu in what is now Nepal, and she was transported to the heavenly palace in the Himalayas where she was cleansed and purified.

Then the spirit of the Buddha appeared to her in the form of a moonlit cloud bearing a lotus which circled her three times before entering her body. At that moment, musical instruments played marvellous music untouched by the fingers of gods or men, trees burst into flower and the rivers stopped flowing in order to see the miracle.

The next morning Mahamaya told her husband what had happened. They both believed it was a dream, and consulted astrologers to find out what it meant. The astrologers told them that they would have a son.
'He will see old age, sickness, death and a hermit and these will have an effect on him so profound that he will leave the kingdom and become a holy man to seek enlightenment. He will eventually discover this and become the

Supreme Buddha—the Enlightened One.'

During her pregnancy, Mahamaya's body was as transparent as a crystal casket so that the infant was always visible inside her. In the tenth month of the moon, she set out for her parents' kingdom since it was the custom for women to give birth in their mothers' homes. However, as she rested in a garden on the way, she gave birth to a baby boy and when he was placed on the ground before his mother, a lotus sprang from the spot. Seven days later, Mahamaya died and the heavy-hearted Sudodhan recalled the prophecy of the astrologers. Terrified that his son would leave him one day, he built three palaces filled with all the pleasures of the world. All mention of illness, poverty and misery were forbidden. The palaces were heavily guarded and the young prince, named Siddharta, never felt the need to leave them. Siddharta grew to manhood with no memory of his previous incarnations and fell in love with and married a beautiful noblewoman called Yashodhara. They lived happily together in the three palaces, but eventually Siddharta began to feel restless and wished to discover what lay beyond their walls.

The king reluctantly agreed to his son's request to go and look, but on the day that Siddharta was to ride out, the king commanded the infirm, ill and poor to stay out of sight so that the young prince would remain ignorant of suffering and pain. However, the gods knew that Siddharta had to fulfil his destiny, and a minor god appeared to Siddharta as a withered old man: his body was crooked with age and illness and he could hardly breathe. Amazed, Siddharta asked Channa his charioteer what this was.

'An old man,' Channa replied and when Siddharta asked the meaning of the word 'old', Channa had to explain.

Another day Siddharta saw a cripple, then a corpse in a funeral procession. When Channa had explained the significance of all these to the prince, he asked 'Must everyone die?'

'Yes,' replied Channa.

The prince was perplexed. What was the point of life if there was no escape from illness, old age and death? As he wondered about this, he saw a yogi begging for alms.

'What are you doing?' he asked the yogi.

'I have forsaken the world,' the yogi explained, 'to seek eternal peace and escape from hatred, lust and the desire for physical comfort.'

'But how can you gain peace from discomfort?' Siddharta asked in confusion.

'Worldly things are short-lived,' replied the yogi. 'By giving them up I hope to attain eternal freedom in another world.'

Siddharta was so deeply affected by the yogi's words that he returned immediately to his palace and told his father that he had decided to lead the life of an ascetic. No arguments from the king and the people could change his mind. Not even the birth of a baby son could weaken his resolve.

One night he summoned his charioteer. 'Prepare my horse Kantak for me,' he commanded, 'I shall leave today to follow my path.'

Channa begged Siddharta to choose instead to become emperor of the world but Siddharta was adamant. For the last time, he went into Yashodhara's room longing to hold her in his arms along with his son, but he knew it would only cause further heartache so he gazed at them tenderly while they lay sleeping, and crept out of the palace. As soon as he mounted Kantak, spirits lifted the horse into the air so that the sound of his hooves would not waken the sleeping kingdom. When they had reached its border, Siddharta dismounted to say farewell to Channa and Kantak and to thank them for serving him so faithfully. Then he walked on alone. On his travels, he met a poor hunter and exchanged his princely robes for the hunter's tattered garments. Now at last he could begin his search for the answer to his question: how can the world be saved from the cycle of birth and death and from suffering and pain.

Siddharta joined two different hermitages but did not find what he was searching for. Then he made his way to a village named Gaya and began to live in the woods nearby. Like other holy men, he denied himself all food except for a few grains of millet seed. Of course, he soon grew weak and thin but he realized that his weakened state was taking him further from his goal instead of towards it and so decided to eat

Seeing that Siddharta was not afraid, Mara retreated and instead sent a message that Siddharta's cousin planned to take over his kingdom—but this news only made Siddharta even more determined to forsake the world of pain and suffering. Then Mara sent his three beautiful daughters to tempt Siddharta but he had no interest in the pleasures they offered. Mara was enraged by the failure of his schemes. Mounting his battle elephant, he hurled his terrifying discus at Siddharta but the weapon, which could split mountains in two, simply flew towards Siddharta and hovered above his head, refusing to harm him. Mara then rode up to Siddharta.

'Leave this place,' he thundered, but the prince answered calmly, 'This seat is mine, I have earned it through many rebirths and much meditation. Why should I give it to you who have no merit?'

'My merit is greater than yours,' Mara shouted and commanded his army to confirm it.

'We bear witness for Mara,' they bellowed but Siddharta knew that their testimony was biased, and he touched the ground and asked it to bear witness truly.

Suddenly the Earth Goddess appeared at his feet in all her magnificence. 'I bear witness for Siddharta,' she pronounced in a voice like a cosmic drum. Terrified and convinced, Mara and his demons fled never to plague Siddharta again.

Siddharta remained for seven days and nights beneath the tree, meditating until he had completely remembered his previous existences and was fully enlightened: the meaning of life and faith became perfectly clear to him and he became the Supreme Buddha.

Forty-nine days later, he set out to preach his message. On his travels, he converted his family and the people of Kapilavastu and over the years he began to accept women into his order as nuns.

For forty-five years he roamed the land, begging and preaching. Then one day he accepted a meal of pork from a devout goldsmith: the meal was infected and the Buddha became ill. Knowing that he was to die soon, the Buddha set out for the city of

and grow strong. At exactly the same time, Sujata the daughter of the village chief dreamed that she should prepare a dish of milk and rice and serve it to the holy man on a golden platter. She did so and Siddharta accepted the food, recognizing the golden platter to be a good omen. Siddharta ate his meal then made his way to a special tree known as the Wisdom Tree. A long procession of birds, beasts and spirits who were attracted by his holiness followed him there.

Meanwhile from the opposite direction, Mara the god of evil was marching against Siddharta with the forces of his hideous army of fire-breathing monsters, man-eating serpents and demons who drank blood and chewed bones. Some had a hundred thousand insatiable mouths and others had clinging, misshapen limbs. They were all armed with clubs, spears and bows and heavily protected by armour. Siddharta saw this terrifying army approaching but serenely continued towards the tree and sat down beneath it, vowing never to rise until he had received complete enlightenment.

Kushinagar, and there he explained to his chief disciple that the goldsmith was not to be blamed, because he had proved that no-one can escape sickness, decay and death. This made his offering as blessed as that of the village girl Sujata.

Then the Buddha lay down on a couch in a grove of trees and sent word to the kings of the surrounding states to come and see him for the last time. Thousands did come and as he passed into Heaven he told them all that even the least among them would attain Heaven if they tried hard enough.

His body was wrapped in the finest of brocades and placed on a funeral pyre, but no-one was able to set it alight. Then suddenly it blazed up of its own accord and when the flames died down again, all that remained was a heap of relics which glittered like diamonds and pearls. The Buddha's cheekbones, teeth and skull are enshrined in magnificent monuments in India even to this day, and his message has spread throughout the world. Today millions of Buddhists follow his teachings.

The Sikhs: Guru Nanak

Sikhism is a major religion from northern India and especially the Punjab. It contains elements of both Hinduism and Islam, and was founded in the sixteenth century AD by Guru Nanak.

Kalu was a clerk who lived in the village of Talvandi, west of Lahore. In 1469, his wife gave birth to a son who was named Nanak. Millions of gods came to see the baby, along with many legendary heroes and wise men.
'A great man has come into the world,' they said. 'Homage shall be paid to him.' This turned out to be an accurate prediction and today the village of Talvandi is called Nankana Sahab in memory of Nanak.

During his childhood Nanak played with the other boys but he was already preoccupied with thoughts about religion. He believed that there was only one true God and wished to know more about him. When he grew up, Nanak married and became the father of two sons, but

he spent all his time in the company of Hindu and Muslim holy men. His family was upset by Nanak's indifference to his work and his enigmatic responses to their advice: his father begged him to concentrate on his training for the family business or at least to look after their farmland, but Nanak took no notice.

Nanak spent so long sleeping, meditating and praying that he forgot to eat for days at a time. When he fell, he forgot to get up, remaining on the ground until someone helped him. Because of this he was often thought to be ill. There were, however, other signs that Nanak was a special man. One day the village chieftain saw him sleeping under a tree. It was the middle of the day and the shadows had disappeared from under the other trees, but Nanak's tree still cast a deep, cool shadow which protected him from the heat of the sun.
'There is no doubt that your son is dear to God in some special way,' the chieftain said to Nanak's father, 'because even nature alters its course for his comfort.'

Nanak continued to live in his own world full of love for the Lord he could not see but often spoke about. Eventually his brother-in-law invited him to come and work for the Nawab of Sultanpur, and Nanak did so. Nanak would spend each night with his admirers who listened to his preachings and sang hymns with him in a ceremony known as *kirtan*. Then each day at dawn he would go, like all pious men, to bathe in the river.

One day after completing *kirtan*, Nanak stepped into the river to bathe and did not resurface for several days. His friends all thought that he had drowned and were astounded when he came back unharmed. Nanak told them that he had been with the Lord who had identified himself as the Supreme Brahma (Creator). Enigmatically, Guru Nanak announced that there was no Hindu or Muslim. There were many differences between the followers of these two religions, and Hindus would not willingly become the disciples of a Muslim religious teacher, nor Muslims of a Hindu one, but both Hindus and Muslims became followers of Guru Nanak so there was no difference between them.

Free to wander, Guru Nanak prepared to leave Sultanpur much to the regret of his employer the Nawab. With him went Mardana, a musician from Nanak's home village who now travelled with him everywhere, playing a string instrument known as the rubab when the Guru wanted to recite a hymn.

One day while travelling with the Guru, Mardana complained how bitterly hungry he felt. The Guru assured him they would eat at the nearest village but Mardana claimed he would die of hunger long before then. So the Guru pointed to a tree and told Mardana to eat as much fruit from it as he wished.

'But do not take any with you,' he commanded. Mardana ate what he could but the fruit was so delicious that he could not resist filling his pockets with more. As they walked on, Mardana suddenly fell down dead. The Guru commanded the corpse to explain what had happened and it replied that Mardana had carried the fruit away with him and eaten it.

'Those berries were poisonous,' explained Guru Nanak. 'I made them edible to satisfy your hunger, but when we left the tree, the fruit became poisonous again.'

He placed his foot on Mardana's forehead and saying a prayer, brought him back to life. But in spite of his experience, Mardana remained very fond of his food, and often complained that the Guru did not bother about his companion's hunger because he himself never felt the pangs of hunger or thirst.

Once the Guru visited a village where no-one would give him shelter except a poor carpenter who slept on the floor, giving his bed to Nanak. When Guru Nanak woke up the next morning, he smashed the front of the house, broke off a large stick from the shattered timber and used it to destroy the bed on which he had slept. Then he left. A disciple named Saido asked why he had punished the only man in the village who had helped him.

'When the carpenter bought the house the four legs of the bed were buried in its floor. Now that the bed is useless, he will have to dig the legs out. He will discover four pots of treasure buried beneath. A palace will be raised from his hovel,' he concluded 'and fine bedsteads will replace the broken one.'

After many years of wandering and preaching, Nanak arrived at the southern shores of the continent and stood beside the waves of the Indian Ocean. His disciples thought that they could go no further but Nanak prayed to God and the waves stopped moving and became as firm as a thick sheet of glass. Nanak told Saido and Siho to walk with him across the ocean to Singhala-Dipa, now know as Sri Lanka. No rain had fallen on the island for many months and all of the trees and plants were turning brown in the fierce heat of the Sun. When they arrived, Guru Nanak entered a large, dried-up garden and sat down to rest. As he did so, the leaves of the trees and bushes turned green and all of the flowers burst into bloom. The gardener ran to tell the owner, Raja Shiv Nabha, that a holy man had come who had revived his garden by his presence. Raja Shiv Nabha hurried to greet him.

'Come to my palace,' he invited, 'and let me honour you properly.' Nanak replied that he would not go on foot. The king offered him the mount of his choice.

'I will ride on the back of a raja,' replied Nanak, 'if there is a raja who is willing.'

'Then climb on my back,' offered Shiv Nabha, 'for I am the raja.'

While his subjects watched, he carried Nanak to his palace. There he presented his wife Chandkala to him.

'What can we offer you to eat?' she asked.

'I am fasting,' Nanak said, 'but if you can find a twelve-year-old prince, I will eat his flesh.'

The king and queen had a son who was exactly twelve years old, and they argued fiercely about him. Chandkala did not wish to sacrifice her son, but finally agreed when her husband insisted that the holy man's wishes should be obeyed. They told the prince what they had decided and he unhesitatingly promised to do whatever Nanak demanded. The prince had been married on his twelfth birthday as was the custom in the kingdom and his young wife loved him dearly but she also accepted the decision and so the prince was presented to Nanak.

'He is no good to me as he is,' replied the holy

man. 'Let his mother hold his head and his wife hold his feet and his father slaughter him with a knife. Then boil his flesh and I shall eat it.'

The parents and the young wife were horrified by his words but obeyed in silence. Nanak next asked the prince's parents and wife to shut their eyes, say 'Vah Guru' (Praise the Lord) and put the flesh in their mouths. Of course they were sickened by the thought, but they did as they were told and when they opened their eyes they saw that the holy man had disappeared and in his place sat their son. Naturally the raja was overjoyed to see his son alive and well but he was also distressed at Nanak's disappearance for he was afraid it meant he had annoyed the Guru. But in fact he had proved his piety by his readiness to sacrifice his beloved son and Guru Nanak accepted the Raja and his family as disciples a year later.

After years of wanderings and many adventures, Guru Nanak went back to settle in Kartarpur near Lahore and stayed there for the last fifteen years of his life. It is now called Dera Baba Nanak which means the settlement of Baba Nanak. Towards the end of his life in 1539, he knew that he would soon die and be united with his beloved Lord. On his last night, he went and sat beneath a dead tree which at once became lush and green again. Surrounded by Hindus and Muslims who sang funeral songs and hymns to him, he passed into a trance. Before the Guru lost consciousness completely, he heard the Hindus and Muslims arguing about his burial.
'We will bury him according to our custom,' said the Muslims.
'We will cremate him according to our custom,' insisted the Hindus.
'Lay flowers on either side of me,' whispered the Guru. 'The group whose flowers are freshest tomorrow can do as they will with my body.'

Near dawn, the Guru passed into eternity and his followers did as he had suggested. Each group put fresh flowers beside him. When they returned the next morning, they found that the Guru's body had disappeared without trace and the flowers of both groups still remained as fresh as ever.

Legends of Sufi saints

Islam is the most important religion of what is now Pakistan and Bangladesh and also has millions of believers in India itself. One branch of it is Sufism which arrived in India in the eleventh century AD. Sufis regard God as all-forgiving and willing to envelop all mankind in His loving embrace, and they think that loving one's neighbours, generosity and kindness please God as much as do formal prayers and services. Many stories have grown up about the holy men of Sufism: one of the most famous saints was Baba Farid, who was born in a town called Kahtwal which is now in Pakistan. He became a disciple of the revered saint Bakhtiar and among his own disciples was Nizamuddin Aulia whose shrine in Delhi is visited every day by thousands of people. Baba Farid lived in poverty for most of his life because although he had many followers who gave him gifts so that he could support himself, Baba Farid gave everything away to the needy.

Baba Farid lived for many years in what is now the city of Pak Pattan, and once fell seriously ill there. When his health showed no sign of improvement he asked his disciple Nizamuddin Aulia and his son to pray for his recovery. That night after saying his prayers, his son had a strange dream. He dreamed he saw a man burying something by a grave and covering it with mud and leaves. In the dream, he moved closer to the grave and realized that it belonged to a famous magician who years before had preyed upon the citizens of the town. He had threatened them with curses and poisons if they did not pay him money and had terrorized the whole city. Finally, however, Baba Farid had overcome him by his prayers and the magician had later died.

When the son awoke the next day he found that his father had grown weaker and was in great pain. The son told Nizamuddin about his dream and said that the man in it had been the magician's son.

As soon as Nizamuddin heard the dream he visited the grave and cleared away the sand which had piled up on it. A few inches below

the surface he found a crude effigy of Baba Farid made of dough. It was wrapped with horse-hair and stuck all over with pins. Nizamuddin flung the effigy in a river and reported the incident to the city's governor. The magician's son was hunted down and arrested.

The governor then took him to Baba Farid to decide on a suitable punishment, but Baba Farid had recovered completely and simply replied, 'I am well now. I pray to God to forgive him. I have forgiven him and so should you.' The magician's son was so overcome by the holy man's compassion that he sincerely repented his sins and became one of Baba Farid's followers.

Minstrels and story-tellers throughout South Asia tell stories of a Sufi saint named Sarvar, whose generosity was famous even in his own lifetime. Sarvar lived with his parents and three step-brothers on their small patch of land in the district of Multan. When his maternal grandfather died, leaving him a vast tract of fertile farming land, Sarvar decided to live there so that he could plough the land more efficiently. His step-brothers were envious of his good fortune and begged him to divide the land into four parts and he agreed, pleased that they wanted to be near him. He even let them make the division. However, the step-brothers kept the best land for themselves and gave him only a barren piece of wasteland. Sarvar was not disturbed. He thanked his step-brothers for

their kindness and began to set to work. His step-brothers laughed at him because he always prayed to God before each day's ploughing and sowing. However, when the harvest came, they were astounded to find that his crops yielded at least ten times more grain than theirs. 'Brother,' they said, 'our crops have failed because we gave you the best land and divided the barren parts amongst ourselves—now we are suffering for our generosity while you benefit from our kindness.'
When Sarvar gladly offered to let them take what they needed from his stocks, they took most of his grain for themselves and left him with only one bin. Sarvar gave even that away to the sick and the poor and lived on what scraps he could find.

Not long afterwards his step-brothers asked him to come with them to the city of Multan to see the governor, whose name was Ghanu. When they had entered the city gates, Sarvar's step-brothers turned to him.
'We have come to pay the land taxes we owe to Governor Ghanu,' they told him.

Sarvar was taken aback. He had not asked his step-brothers why they were making the journey and he had no money to pay his taxes. Anxiously, he prayed to God to save him from humiliation. They had hardly entered the city when an enormous crowd gathered around Sarvar, attracted by his air of holiness.

Governor Ghanu was watching from his palace and realized that a saint must have arrived in Multan.

'I will see whether this is a real saint,' he thought for there were many pretenders about. He sent Sarvar an empty pitcher and bowl on a covered tray. 'Welcome the saint,' he told his servant, 'and offer him some refreshment with my greetings.'

The embarrassed servant did as the governor had told him. Sarvar thanked him, raised the cloth—and ate the rice and milk which had miraculously appeared there. His step-brothers ate too and the bowl and pitcher were returned still full to the governor with Sarvar's blessings. The governor was now convinced that Sarvar was genuinely a saint, and gave him a hundred thousand gold coins, a magnificent stallion and a priceless robe of honour. He discovered that Sarvar's step-brothers were jealous of him and would try to harm him if they could, so he threw them into prison. However, Sarvar immediately went to the prison and asked the jailer to free the prisoners. The jailer handed him the key to his step-brothers' cell, but that was not enough for Sarvar—he wanted to open all the cells.

'I love them all as brothers,' he said. 'I pray for the freedom of them all.'

Governor Ghanu was consulted.

'If the saint wishes it,' he replied, 'they shall all go free.'

Sarvar's next mission was to visit the food and cloth merchants of the city. He gave them all of his money and said, 'Feed, clothe and shelter the poor as long as this money lasts.'

Then he set out for home. As he left the city, he met a small group of men about to enter it. 'We are pilgrims who have fasted many years and are going to find food in the city,' the told him, 'but we have no money.'

Sympathetically, Sarvar handed them the robe and horse which Ghanu had given him. 'Sell them,' he said, 'and buy food and clothes.' However, when the pilgrims tried to sell the robe and horses the townspeople at once recognized them as the governor's gifts and were afraid to buy them in case it caused them trouble, so Sarvar asked the pilgrims to slaughter and eat the horse and to make clothes out of the robe. Seizing the chance to discredit him with Ghanu, his step-brothers made their way back to Governor Ghanu.

'Sarvar has no regard for your generous gifts,' they told him. 'He slaughtered the horse and ripped up the robe.'

Incensed, the governor sent a messenger to demand the return of his gifts. Sarvar fell to his knees and prayed to God.

'Do not humiliate me Lord,' he pleaded, 'I must return the gifts to their owner.'

Miraculously, the horse and robe reappeared, and Sarvar himself rode the horse back to the city to return the gifts to Ghanu, who was once more convinced of Sarvar's holiness.

'Marry my daughter, Sarvar,' he asked. At first Sarvar declined, saying he was a poor man and could not look after her, but after some persuasion he agreed. A date was arranged and on the wedding day, Ghanu fed thousands of poor people because he knew it would please Sarvar.

After the marriage ceremony, the musicians who were about to play for the guests begged Sarvar to give them a magic fruit called pilu fruit.

'It is said to sweeten the voice of all who eat it.' they said, 'We beg you to give us some so that we can make music that will enchant the bride and the guests.'

It was winter and not even ordinary fruit grew on the trees let alone magic ones. Sarvar looked hopelessly out of the window at the bare trees and told the musicians he could not do as they wanted. Still they begged and pleaded. Sarvar longed to fulfil their wishes and a silent prayer went out of his heart that they should get what they wanted. Suddenly, in full view of the guests, a tree directly outside the window began to sprout new shoots. Within moments the shoots had bloomed, the magic pilu fruit had grown and ripened and the musicians were able to pick and eat their fill.

Sarvar and his bride lived happily together from that day onward, and throughout his life, God provided Sarvar with wealth and riches, for Sarvar never kept it for himself and through him God's bounties always reached the needy.

Shiv, god of destruction

The great god Shiv who lived in his heaven on the snowy peaks of Mount Kailash was a god of many moods. When dealing with evil creatures, he took pleasure in destruction. He was also lord of goblins, demons and restless wandering spirits. He haunted cemeteries and cremation grounds and wore a crown of serpents and a necklace of skulls. He hated being disobeyed and trampled furiously on the heads of rebellious demons. Shiv frightened even the other gods, who criticized him for his macabre ways—chief among his critics was Daksha, the father of Man. Yet Shiv was also greatly loved, because death is simply a stage in the cycle of creation and represents release and rebirth just as winter is followed by spring. So Shiv was 'Mahadev' (which means the Restorer) as well as the Destroyer.

Like many of the Hindu gods, Shiv can change his appearance, and sometimes he has four arms and five heads with which to watch every part of the world. He is always very beautiful with a light skin and a third eye on his forehead which has terrible power when Shiv becomes enraged. When the world was being created the many things that were to live in it were thrown up from the churning ocean of milk. The ocean's first gift was the divine cow Surabhi whose son Nandi, the snow-white bull, later became Shiv's constant companion. The second gift was a crescent moon which he snatched from the waves and placed on his forehead to decorate his hair; there it glowed for ever more. The third thing to come from the ocean was a deadly draught of poison and this Shiv drank in order to save the world from harm. Instead of swallowing it, he held it in his neck and the strength of its venom turned his neck blue.

Once Shiv decided to visit Earth in the shape of a man to punish a group of ascetics who had become unbelievers and spoke of a world without gods. Their wives fell in love with Shiv's great beauty as soon as they saw him even though they did not know who he was. The ascetics became jealous and using their combined powers, produced a tiger which leaped out at Shiv from their sacrificial fires. Shiv simply caught the tiger with one hand, peeled off its skin and slung it over his body as a shawl.

Next the ascetics caused a large deer to pounce on him. Shiv fielded it with another of his four hands and held it there ever after. Still determined to destroy him, the ascetics created a vicious serpent but, being himself the Lord of Serpents, Shiv hung the creature round his neck as a necklace. Finally the ascetics created a hideous dwarf-demon who flailed at Shiv with a club which had a skull at one end. Shiv took away the club and held it in his third hand. He then pinned the dwarf-demon down with his foot.

Shiv was furious by this time and he began slowly to perform his celestial dance. This dance represents his five functions—Creation, Preservation, Destruction, Embodiment and Release, and it is said to cause the movement of the universe. Gradually, the momentum of Shiv's dance built up to a frenzied climax and the heretical ascetics and all the other creatures who watched its power were carried away by its beauty. It is said that they gave up everything in this and many other re-incarnations for the promise of seeing it once more.

After this visit to Earth, three of Shiv's hands were permanently occupied by the tiger's skin, the deer and the demon's club. In the fourth, he held his bow or when meditating, a drum shaped like an hourglass as a symbol that he continued to be the patron of devout ascetics.

How Ganga came to Earth

Shiv spent much time in meditation to ensure that all went well with the world, that good deeds were rewarded and evil ones were avenged. One day he was deep in meditation when he became aware that King Bhagirath was calling to him. Shiv knew that King Bhagirath was a saintly man who had given up his kingdom and spent years praying to him. Shiv also knew that he would not ask for anything selfish so the god stirred from the tiger-skin on which he was sitting and descended to Earth to the place where the king sat praying.
'I am pleased with you Bhagirath,' said the Lord of Creation in a melodious voice. 'Do not be afraid to tell me what you want.'

Bhagirath fell down at Shiv's feet, crying tears of gratitude. 'Lord Mahadev,' he said humbly, 'I cannot believe my good fortune in being honoured by your presence.' Then he began to tell Shiv his story.

More than a hundred thousand years ago, his ancestor King Sagar had decided to perform an important sacrifice which required a special horse to be consecrated at a ritual feast and then set free to wander wherever it wished for a year. Sagar commanded his 60,000 sons to follow the horse and, in accordance with the custom, ordered them to conquer the kings of every country the horse entered. But the princes lost sight of the horse and their angry father told them not to return home until they had found it. The princes searched all over the world and finally dug a massive gorge to the underworld: the gorge was so large that eventually it covered more than half the world and when the princes climbed down into it and entered the underworld, they found the horse grazing peacefully in a meadow. Nearby the great sage Kapila sat deep in meditation and the 60,000 princes at once accused him of stealing the sacrificial horse.

Kapila was enraged both by the accusation and by the interruption to his prayers. According to some, Kapila was the son of Agni the fire-god, and now he angrily glared at the princes and a sacred flame leaped from his eyes which instantly burned them to ashes. Many years later, a nephew of the dead princes named Ansumat discovered their remains lying beside Kapila who was still deep in meditation. Ansumat fell at Kapila's feet and begged that the remains of the princes be washed in holy water so that their souls could enter Heaven. Kapila agreed on condition that the river goddess Ganga came down to Earth to cleanse them. He prophesied that a descendant of Ansumat would be the one to make this come about and now Bhagirath had finally succeeded in invoking Shiv to ask his help.

Ganga had been born from Vishnu's toe and was an unstable creature as is the nature of water. Once, long ago, the gods had begged Shiv to sing his celestial song. Vishnu knew its stupendous force, and had decided to sit directly in front of Shiv and absorb part of the

might of his song which could otherwise have caused great destruction in the universe. As Shiv's song became louder, Ganga was hypnotized by its beauty and began to rise and become fuller. She would have flooded the Heavens in her ecstasy but fortunately Vishnu was prepared and imprisoned her in a large pot before she could do any damage. Ever since then she had been annoyed with Shiv for having such an effect on her.

'I will grant your wish,' Shiv told Bhagirath. 'But the might of Ganga gushing down to Earth would be too immense for the land to bear. There would be earthquakes, floods and fire, and the crops would be ruined for years to come. So I will sit in the spot where she is to fall and bear the impact of her power on my head. Then, when she has landed, you can take her to the remains of your ancestors and your years of prayer to me will have been repaid.'

Shiv seated himself beside Bhagirath among the Himalayan glaciers and willed Ganga to make her appearance. Ganga could not resist the power of his will but was furious at being ordered to descend from Heaven. Since she had an old score to settle with Shiv she decided that she would wash him away in her swirling

currents. She cascaded down from the sky as a mighty waterfall, but Shiv was prepared for her tricks—he grew into a giant and imprisoned her in the matted locks of his hair. She flowed in and out of his hair for many years and by the time she reached Earth she was harmlessly split into seven streams.

Acting on Shiv's advice, King Bhagirath blew a loud, clear note on a horn and led the way to the great gorge where the ashes of the princes lay. The main stream followed the sound, winding in and out of many countries and villages until she finally came to the entrance to the underworld. There she flooded into the vast gap which covered more than half the world and filled it to the brim, washing the remains of Bhagirath's ancestors in her holy waters. The great river is today known as the sacred River Ganges or Mother Ganga, and the great gorge was named Sagar after the king whose sons had dug it. And that is what it is still called to this day, for from that day onward *sagar* came to mean 'ocean'.

Daksha's sacrifice

One day as Shiv and his beautiful wife Sati sat talking in his heaven Kailash, Sati noticed a large procession passing by. Curious, she asked her husband where the gods were going.

'To the grand sacrifice to be held by Daksha, your father,' replied Shiv. Sati was amazed.

'Then why have you not been invited?' she demanded angrily. 'You should have been the first to be asked.'

Shiv smiled gently at his wife's loyalty and fervour.

'Daksha has always been hostile to me,' he explained. 'Once long ago, I was deep in meditation at a sacrificial fire when he passed by me. Being profoundly involved in my thoughts, I did not greet him. I was already his son-in-law and since then he has resented me for what he considers my lack of respect.'

Sati's incredulity increased. 'Does my father not realize that you are the Supreme Creator and that no-one can equal you?'

49

'You are a good and true wife Sati,' Shiv replied gently, 'but Daksha thinks differently—he, too, is a creator and was responsible for the birth of mankind and other creatures. That is why he sees me as a rival.'

'Invited or not,' Sati said furiously, 'I think we should go. It is after all my own father's house and I at least need no invitation.'

'Then go with my blessings Sati,' replied the Lord of Creation, 'but do not forget that Daksha will shower insults upon your husband. You must be strong enough to bear them in silence and not allow your rage to show in your father's presence. If you are unable to tolerate his insults, I fear you may come to harm.'

Taking Nandi, the gentle white bull who was Shiv's companion and mount, Sati arrived at her father's grand sacrifice.

'Welcome, my daughter,' her father said. 'I am glad you have seen fit to leave my brutish son-in-law behind.'

'My lord is deep in meditation, father,' said Sati, remembering her husband's warning. 'I came alone.'

Daksha laughed and speaking in a loud voice began to condemn Shiv, calling him the demon

of death and an impious haunter of cremation grounds.

'What place has the goblin lord of witches and foul spirits in a sacred ceremony such as mine?' he boomed.

Sati was hurt by his insults to her husband and begged her father to stop but Daksha was so pleased with the idea that his son-in-law knew every holy man and god had been invited to the sacrifice except himself, that he could not contain himself.

'It is disgraceful for a so-called god to wear filthy rags, cover himself with snakes and dance like a madman at ceremonies. I have never understood why my own daughter went to such pains to win a creature like that for her husband. You are after all, the grand-daughter of the Supreme Spirit Brahma himself—for as you know, I sprang from his right thumb and your mother from his left. How then can Shiv consider himself greater than I?'

Sati could stand her father's insults no longer. She looked around her and saw that everyone was horrified by Daksha's words but no-one would meet her eye or defend her husband from Daksha's slanders. Trembling with rage (for she had an earth-shaking fury of her own) she looked directly at her father.

'If you are unable to hold your tongue,' she said in a thunderous voice, 'and disgrace yourself so shamefully in the presence of thousands, including those who have devoted their lives to my husband; if you can shout insults at the Supreme Creator with your sacrificial fires lit and your priests chanting incantations to lesser gods, then I am too ashamed to be known as your daughter. My husband has instructed me not to take any revenge upon anyone present, much less you—so I merely denounce you before this assembly. I shall consume myself in a fire and return to the womb of the Earth until I am born again to a father whom I can respect.' As she spoke, a fierce flame appeared beneath Sati and burned her to ashes.

'Continue with the sacrifice!' Daksha ordered the open-mouthed priests. 'Many like her come and go all the time. The grand sacrifice will not be interrupted for her.' But Nandi had already returned to Shiv and told him of Sati's death.

When Shiv heard that his beloved wife was dead, he gave a mighty roar that shook Heaven and Earth. Then he threw his blazing trident to the ground and trampled on it, creating from it a magnificent and powerful demon named Vira-bhadra. To accompany him Shiv conjured up an army of demons and demi-gods who descended like a hurricane on Daksha's feast, destroying the sacrificial offering and killing all those who dared defend Daksha.

Indra, who was there to accept his portion of the sacrifice, leaped to his feet to protect himself but was easily knocked down by Vira-bhadra. Other guests had their eyes pulled out and their noses cut off. Vahni, fire itself, had its limbs severed. In the battle, Daksha was beheaded and when one of the holy men had his beard shaved off, the others realized they must finally stand up for what was right and walked over to Shiv's side to seek refuge with him.

They tried to calm him but Shiv still quivered and shook with wrath and grief at the loss of Sati. As he shook, a tremor ran through the womb of the Earth, mountains tottered, the winds howled and ripped massive trees out by their roots. Then Vishnu himself arrived, followed by the great four-headed god Brahma and their wives. They soothed the furious god and pleaded with him to forgive Daksha. Relenting, Shiv brought back to life all the people who had been killed in the battle and cured all those who had been injured. Finally he looked up, suppressing the power of his destructive third eye.

'I will grant Brahma and Vishnu their wish,' he stated. 'Daksha too will be returned to life, but he must bear the mark of his foolishness forever.' The gods agreed to Shiv's condition and Daksha was revived: the mark of his foolishness was clear for all to see for instead of his own head, he wore the head of a goat. In spite of this, Daksha fell at Shiv's feet weeping with gratitude, and finally acknowledged that Shiv was greater than he.

With a mighty effort Shiv contained his grief for the loss of Sati, and he fell into profound meditation, waiting for the time when she would be reincarnated as Parvati and be his wife once more.

Ganesh, god of good luck

One day after Sati had been reborn as Parvati and was once more married to Shiv, she spent a particularly long time in prayer. When she stood up, she discovered that her skin was dry and her body stiff, so she went to bathe in a lake that lay high among the peaks of Kailash. As she washed the dust from her body, it began to form into a large, round shape which eventually grew into a beautiful baby boy. Parvati hugged the child delightedly and took him back to see his father Shiv.
'We will call him Ganesh,' declared his father and made him Lord of the Ganas, a troop of demi-gods who were Shiv's attendants.

Parvati, too, was proud of her child and decreed that he would be the remover of all obstacles. Then all the other gods and goddesses gave him their blessings. Sarasvati, goddess of wisdom, gave him wisdom and learning, while Lakshmi, goddess of good fortune, blessed him with the power to bring good luck.

As he grew up, Ganesh became a benevolent and cheerful god, gentle and humble in general but full of mischief and with a tendency to boastfulness. One day a famous wise man named Dwaipayana came to Ganesh and asked him to write down an epic which he intended to dictate. Mischievously, Ganesh replied, 'Anyone can write what you dictate. If I am to be the one, you must create something exceptional and worthy of me. If you can dictate it without stopping or pausing even once, then I will write it down.'

The wise man agreed, then embarked on a vast work about the dynasties which were to come from his sons Dhritashastra and Pandu and the rivalries which would exist among them. The epic, which became known as the *Mahabharat*, is the longest work of poetry in the world, with ninety thousand verses of thirty lines each. Its writer also arranged the great books known as the *Vedas*. From then on, worshippers prayed to Ganesh before the writing of any book, before the start of any important business venture and most especially for anything to do with learning and education.

Ganesh is small and heavily built with a pendulous stomach which can contain unlimited quantities of food. His body is sometimes red or pink but at other times bright yellow. He usually rides on a rat and his four arms hold a club, a discus, a shell and a water-lily. He has the head of an elephant because he once enraged his father. It happened like this.

One day his mother Parvati went to have a bath and asked him to guard her bath-chamber. 'Allow no-one in,' she commanded and Ganesh settled himself outside the door to do as he was told. Suddenly Shiv arrived and was about to enter. Without stopping to think, Ganesh leaped to his feet and told his father that Parvati did not wish to be disturbed. Enraged that his own son should oppose him, Shiv drew his sword and cut off Ganesh's head. It flew into the universe where it is still spinning from the strength of the blow. Parvati heard the disturbance outside and came out to find her much loved and loyal son lying headless on the ground. Her grief and fury knew no bounds and Shiv, too, began to regret his rash act. To placate her, Shiv sent a thousand goblins, demons and imps to look for the head of a male child to replace that of Ganesh. Shiv's creatures searched all through the night but each male child that they found was asleep facing his mother and they did not have the heart to remove his head. Then at last they came upon a baby elephant who was sleeping with his head turned away from his mother since otherwise his trunk and his mother's got in the way and prevented them snuggling close together. Immediately Shiv's creatures removed his head and brought it to Shiv. He placed it on Ganesh's shoulders and as Ganesh revived, it sprouted two glorious ivory tusks.

Another legend tells how one of these tusks was lost. Parasu-Ram (the sixth incarnation of the god Vishnu) was a worshipper of Shiv and had been sent to Earth to destroy an evil king. Shiv protected him when he was a child, taught him how to use weapons, and also gave him an axe, or *parasu*, after which he was named. Parasu-Ram grew up to be a mighty warrior with a fierce temper. One day he arrived in Kailash to visit Shiv. Shiv was asleep and Ganesh was reluctant to allow anyone to

disturb him. Politely he asked Parasu-Ram to wait, but the warrior took Ganesh's suggestion as an insult and started a fight.

At first Ganesh twisted his trunk around Parasu-Ram and flung him in the air so that he whirled about and then came crashing down, unconscious. When he revived, he threw his axe at Ganesh, and Ganesh recognized it as the one that Shiv had given to Parasu-Ram. Quickly Ganesh decided that it was not his place to resist a blow from a weapon blessed by his father and he quietly allowed the axe to strike off one of his tusks. Ever since then he has been shown in his portraits with only one tusk.

Ganesh was known for his great loyalty to his parents and was often sent into the world to teach lessons in humility to mortals who were growing arrogant. But he is best known for being the remover of obstacles and the bringer of good luck and is still worshipped before important undertakings.

The eye-saint

A young hunter lived in the hills of south-eastern India. One day, as he returned after catching a great boar, he noticed a shrine adorned by the image of Shiv. As he looked at the face of the image, he felt a deep conviction that he had returned to a much loved parent after many years apart. As he gazed adoringly at the statue's face, he saw that it had been decorated with fresh flowers and sprinkled with clean water from a nearby stream. A traditional offering of fresh fruit and milk lay at its feet. 'Let me also make an offering to my lord,' thought the hunter.

He returned to his camp with the boar and ordered it to be roasted immediately. As soon as it was cooked, he chose the tenderest parts of its flesh, tasting them to ensure they were soft. Then, taking as much as his hands would hold, he ran down to the stream to fetch some water. When he arrived, he realized he would not be able to carry any water since his hands were full. Stooping low, he filled his mouth with water and made his way to a place which he knew was filled with flowering trees. As he passed, he entangled his hair in the branches of the trees, hoping to trap some wild flowers to complete the offering.

Finally he arrived at the shrine. He laid the meat at Shiv's feet, sprinkled the water from his mouth over him and pulled the bruised flowers from his hair to lay before him. Then he drew his bow and arrow and settled there for the night to protect the shrine from danger. At sunrise he went in search of more offerings.

Soon after he had left an old Brahmin priest arrived to tend the shrine as usual. He was horrified to see the dirty water, the bitten meat and the withered flowers. He fell to his knees before the image.
'My lord Shiv,' he cried, 'why have you allowed your shrine to be defiled in this manner?'

The statue of Shiv smiled. 'Do not misunderstand the coarse offerings of this ignorant man. He knows nothing of your sacred rites but what he does is above reproach for he does it with sincerity and love.' Then Shiv asked the Brahmin to return that night and hide behind him to witness the strength of the young man's devotion.

When night came, the young man returned and repeated all the actions he had performed before. When he had finished, he began again to gaze at the face of the statue and this time saw to his horror that one of its eyes was bleeding. He tried to staunch the blood with herbs that were growing nearby, but the blood continued to pour out of the statue's eye. The hunter thought hard. Somewhere he had heard that like cured like. Searching for his sharpest arrow, he cut his own eye out and placed it in the bleeding hollow of the statue's eye. Immediately the bleeding stopped, but no sooner had one eye stopped bleeding than the other started. The hunter pulled out another arrow and was about to cut out his other eye when the statue of Shiv reached out a hand. 'You have proved your love,' he said, 'and won a seat by my side in Kailash.'

The Brahmin realized for the first time in his life that real love could be greater than sacred ritual and the hunter became known all over South India as *Kan-Appan*—'the Eye-Saint'.

The many forms of Vishnu

Vishnu's name comes from the Hindu word *vish* which means 'to pervade', and this fits Vishnu well since his presence is everywhere, and he is able to stride across the whole universe in just three steps. Vishnu is the most widely worshipped of all the Hindu gods and the vast plains of North India are dominated by temples dedicated to him.

In the Hindu religious book called the *Bhagavad Gita* Vishnu says, 'Whenever the sacred law fails and evil raises its head, I take embodied birth to guard the righteous, to root out sinners, and to establish the sacred law. I am born from age to age.' He came to Earth on ten different occasions to preserve the world, each time appearing in the shape of a different creature because it would be dangerous for people to see him in his full brilliance. His most important incarnations were as Ram and Krishna whose stories are told in separate chapters: the story of his first five incarnations are told here.

Manu Vaivaswat was the son of Surya the god of the Sun, and when the world was young he was sent to fill the Earth with all manner of living things because of a curse from his father. One day he was ritually washing himself by the river when he found a tiny fish in the hollow of his palm.

'Save me, Manu,' the fish implored, 'for big fish eat little fish and I am so tiny that I have very little chance of surviving if I stay in the river.'

Manu felt sorry for the little creature so he scooped it out of the river and placed it in an earthenware jar full of water. Soon Matsya the fish had grown so big that Manu had to dig a trench for it. In a few days it grew too large even for the trench.

'Take me to the ocean, Manu,' the fish said. 'There I shall be free from danger.'

Manu did as he was asked and as he released the fish into the ocean, Matsya told him that one year soon a great flood would submerge the world.

'Build a ship in preparation for that year,' Matsya told Manu, 'and pay me homage. When the water starts to rise, take refuge in the ship and I will come to save you.'

Manu thanked the fish and watched him swim away. He was convinced that this was no ordinary fish and began to make a ship as he had advised, and at the end of each day he also prayed to the fish Matsya. The flood came in precisely the year that Matsya had said, and Manu hurriedly boarded the ship to wait for Matsya to come and save him, all the time praising his wisdom and offering thanks for his protection.

Then, as the storm grew fiercer and the ocean began to swell all around him, Manu saw the thundering, roaring mass of water become tranquil for the briefest moment as Matsya approached. He was now a huge fish with a single horn and golden scales.

'Tie the cable of your ship to my horn, Manu,' he instructed and then began to swim further into the waters, drawing the ship behind him.

Soon nothing remained above water except Matsya, Manu's ship and the sky. Matsya swam tirelessly for several years until at last they reached the northern mountain of Hemavat

whose top half still remained proudly above the flood.

'Now tether yourself to this noble mountain,' Matsya ordered. 'You will be lowered gently to the ground when the flood ebbs away. Before I leave, I must bless you and bid you a final farewell, because you will not see me again. I am Vishnu the Preserver. I appeared to you in the shape of a fish to protect you from the deluge; you are destined to start new races to inhabit the world, for you are its only survivor.'

Then Matsya vanished and Manu was left alone to create new plants, animals and people.

Now Vishnu, the all-pervading spirit of the universe, was ready for his sleep, which lasts for thousands of millions of years between each of his successive creations of the universe. He summoned the magnificent cosmic serpent Vasuki, whose body is his couch and whose seven hooded and jewelled heads are his canopy, and the goddesses Lakshmi and Sarasvati prepared his bed. Then Vishnu stretched himself out on his back and sank into slumber in the great cosmic waters.

The churning of the Ocean

Vishnu will never perish and is always merciful and good: it is his function to ensure the triumph of good over evil, so when the gods once found that they had been weakened by a curse put on their king Indra by a quick-tempered sorcerer, they made their way along the shores of the Ocean of Milk to Vishnu's heaven of Vaikuntha to ask his help. They saw a magnificently dazzling light as they approached Vaikuntha, for its outer walls were made of pure gold, and its buildings were carved from gems. The Ganges flowed into Vaikuntha from above, flashing and dancing like a vast belt of crystal before flowing downward to form a magnificent, sparkling river. There were five enormous lakes filled with red, blue and yellow lotuses which scented the air with their subtle fragrance.

Vishnu was sitting on a throne as radiant as the Sun. He was a youth of exquisite beauty: small and lithe and a soft grey-blue. He wore yellow robes and had four arms. The upper two held a conch-shell and his all-powerful discus made by the celestial architect Vishvakarma from the rays he once trimmed off Surya the Sun god. His club was in his third hand and in the fourth there was a lotus blossom. His bow was slung over one shoulder and a sword hung from his belt. An exquisite jewel decorated one of his powerful wrists.

The other gods stood before his throne and all bowed down before him. Then they explained their problem.

'You must go to the Ocean of Milk,' Vishnu told them. 'Throw into it offerings of potent herbs from the three worlds. When you have done this, churn the Ocean as a dairy-maid churns butter with a stick and a rope. Your churning-stick will be Mandar the mountain and your rope the Serpent-King Vasuki. I will help you to stir up the waters, but you must also persuade the giants of Danav to help you. I know that they are your enemies, but you will need their strength. The churning will cause a great deal of disturbance, and the Ocean will throw up many gifts from its depths but the one you need most will be the nectar of life. When

the Ocean has thrown this up, you must drink it and it will restore your strength so your troubles will be over.'

The gods looked at each other doubtfully and finally Indra the king of the gods spoke to Vishnu.

'Thank you for your help,' he said, 'but when the Danav giants drink the nectar of life it will not only give them strength, it will also give them immortality. They will become even stronger than we are and will surely conquer us.'

'Do not worry about that,' Vishnu replied with a smile. 'Promise them they may take what they can and I promise you that they will not drink the nectar of life.'

The gods were reassured and did exactly as Vishnu had told them. They agreed to share the nectar of life with the Danavs and the giants helped wind the serpent Vasuki around Mount Mandar. Slowly the gods and the giants began to churn the Ocean. The gods pulled the snake one way then the Danavs pulled the other and soon the mountain was spinning to and fro making huge waves where before there had been flat sea. The friction between the mountain and the snake created so much heat that it burned up all the trees and plants on the mountain's slopes and nearly boiled the Ocean itself, but Indra commanded rain to fall and cool the mountain down.

By now the heavy mountain was spinning so very quickly that it was boring deep into the Earth, and indeed seemed about to break through it. Vishnu, however, transformed himself into a gigantic tortoise and crawled underneath the mountain so that it rested on his unbreakable shell and could not destroy the world. So great is the power of Vishnu, that even while supporting the mountain he was also able to be seated on the mountain top in his full glory. And from there he encouraged the gods and Danavs in their efforts.

First, the Ocean threw up the sacred cow Surabhi who could grant all wishes. Then came Varuni, goddess of wine, followed by Parijata, the paradise tree which makes the world fragrant. The gods and Danavs churned the waters even more vigorously until the whole Ocean became a mighty whirlpool, and the Apsarases emerged from its depths. The Apsarases are beautiful nymphs and they were taken by Indra to dance before him in his palace. Next the Ocean threw up the moon followed by a deadly poison; Shiv quickly sucked it up to prevent the Danavs misusing it. What poison remained was claimed by the snake gods. Then, seated on a lotus flower, came the goddess Lakshmi. Last of all came Dhanvantri, the divine physician, holding in his hands the cup which contained the nectar of life.

This was the moment for which the gods and the Danavs had been waiting and for an instant they all stood quite still. Then all at once, everyone hurried towards the nectar of life. Only Vishnu stood back and watched. It seemed certain that the Danavs would seize the cup first and keep it for themselves, since the gods were too weakened by the curse to prevent it. However, Vishnu transformed himself into a tantalizing woman and moved in front of the giants. The mysterious woman's beauty was so bewitching that the Danavs were lured away and the gods were able to drink deeply undisturbed; soon they had all regained their strength and powers and were once again ready to begin their eternal war against evil and injustice, much humbler and wiser for their experience.

Vishnu and the demons

Hiranyaksha and Hiranyakashipu were twin brothers who were chiefs of a tribe of giant demons known as the Daityas. The Daityas frequently left their otherworld home to cause havoc on Earth and in one of their terrifying campaigns, Hiranyaksha and his giants dragged the world to the bottom of the cosmic Ocean: some say that this was the cause of the great flood.

Vishnu saw what had happened and turned himself into a wild boar. Wild boars have an excellent sense of smell and Vishnu dived beneath the waves and followed the Earth's scent until he found it, then fought Hiranyaksha for possession of it. The battle raged for more than a thousand years until finally Vishnu destroyed Hiranyaksha and, still in the form of a boar, swam back to the surface of the Ocean carrying the Earth between his tusks.

Now Hiranyakashipu, the remaining twin, began to scheme for revenge against Vishnu and all of his worshippers. For many years he prayed to Shiv, the patron god of all goblins and demons, and in return Shiv made him so immensely powerful that Hiranyakashipu was able to drive Indra from his kingdom and become the ruler of the universe himself. Hiranyakashipu could now do whatever he wanted, and to avenge his twin brother's death he persecuted everyone who worshipped Vishnu. Then one day he was told that his own son Prahlad was one of Vishnu's followers. Hiranyakashipu threatened him with many cruel tortures if he would not end his devotions to Vishnu, but Prahlad would not be persuaded. 'I cannot change, father,' he replied simply. 'I know that Vishnu is the Supreme Being, that Vishnu is in everything, and that our salvation lies in worshipping him. How then can I stop doing so?'
'Then prepare for death,' roared Hiranyakashipu, 'for no son of mine shall worship the one who killed my own flesh and blood.'

Hiranyakashipu ordered his Daitya armies to attack and kill his own son, but Vishnu knew everything that he planned and prevented their weapons from harming him. Then Hiranyakashipu ordered serpents to sting Prahlad with their poisonous fangs, and mighty elephants to trample him and gore him with their massive tusks. Still Prahlad survived unscathed, and with each unexpected victory against his father's forces he became ever more convinced of the power of Vishnu.

By now Hiranyakashipu was immensely frustrated and he went to his sister, the demoness Holika to ask for her help. 'My disgraceful son Prahlad has survived all my efforts to destroy him,' he told her, 'but he would be more vulnerable if he was attacked by someone unexpected. Then he would have no time to save himself with his magical tricks.'

Holika agreed to help and invited Prahlad to visit her. As soon as his back was turned, she tried to burn him up with fire but once again Prahlad was protected by the power of Vishnu. At last Hiranyakashipu gave up and sent Prahlad away from court.

By now the youth was so overwhelmed by the power of Vishnu that he not only worshipped him but preached his virtues to everyone he met. Hiranyakashipu soon heard about his son's missionary activities and ordered Prahlad to return for a final contest. 'You say that Vishnu is everywhere,' he stormed. Then pointing towards a stone pillar, he asked rudely. 'Tell me, is he present in that?' 'Even when unseen, he is present in all things,' Prahlad said quietly.

'Then let him take this,' the demon swore and kicked the pillar violently.

Prahlad cried out in protest but as he did so a mighty lion-headed man leaped out of the pillar, gave an ear-splitting roar and tore Hiranyakashipu to shreds before the eyes of the whole court. To everyone's amazement, he then identified himself as Vishnu in his fourth incarnation, gently embraced Prahlad, and disappeared back into the pillar. Prahlad became the new chief of the Daityas and reigned wisely, returning everything that his father had seized including Indra's kingdom. At the end of his life, he was taken to Paradise and finally achieved eternal peace with his beloved Vishnu.

The giant and the dwarf

After the Danav giants had been tricked out of drinking the nectar of life by Vishnu, they were so furious that they waged war on the gods for many centuries. The gods had regained all of their former power but the Danavs were still formidable enemies, and Bali their leader led the armies of Danav giants to many victories over the gods. Eventually he had conquered most of the kingdoms and heavens of the gods and driven them into retreat. Lastly he and his armies besieged Indra's heaven.

Terrified, the gods begged Vishnu to come and save them. Vishnu again agreed to help and for the fifth time he was reborn on Earth: this time as a dwarf called Vaman.

Vaman went to Bali's camp and asked to see him.

'Why have you come here, little man?' the giant asked.

'I want to find out how generous you are,' the dwarf said cheekily. 'Can you give me what I want? Or perhaps you do not really have the power to do so?'

'I am the master of the three worlds of the Earth, Heaven and Sky,' roared Bali in amusement. 'I can give you whatever I want. Ask anything you like.'

'Then give me all the territory I can cover in three steps,' replied Vaman.

Bali laughed, not in the least worried about losing land worth three of the dwarf's tiny steps. He laughed too soon, however, for Vaman took one gigantic step which covered the whole Earth, a second which covered the Heavens and a third which covered the Sky. Nothing was left for Bali but the lower regions of Hell and, realizing that he had been honourably defeated by someone more powerful than himself, he descended into them.

The other Danavs were no match for the gods now that Bali no longer led them and they were soon defeated. All the kingdoms and heavens of the gods which the Danav king had conquered were returned to them and Vishnu was able to rest again on the back of the cosmic serpent, Vasuki, floating peacefully in the great cosmic waters.

The adventures of Ram

In the dark and deep forests of Banda near Bundelkhand lived a small family. The father fed them by killing the birds and animals around him, and he would not hesitate to kill an animal even if it had little ones to look after. Whenever he had the chance he robbed passers-by without a second thought, attacking children, pilgrims and travellers alike. One day, as he was out hunting, the robber saw seven holy men coming towards him.

'Stop!' he commanded, 'and give me everything you possess.'

'What do you hope to get from holy men who care little for material things?' they asked.

'This is the only way I can support my family,' the robber explained.

'Your wife and children share the fruits of your sins,' said one of them. 'Will they share your punishment too?'

'Of course they will,' the robber answered confidently.

'Then go and ask them,' advised the holy man.

'I will,' responded the robber, 'but if this is a trick to escape, make no mistake. I will track you down and get your riches.'

The robber went off to put the question to his family, little knowing that these men were the Sapta-rishi, the seven great sages who had been born from the forehead of Brahma the Creator and who had unlimited wisdom and power. It was not long before the robber returned to the holy men, miserable and ashamed.

'They will not share my guilt, though they share the results of it,' he told them. 'What can I do to redeem myself?'

'Sit here and repeat the syllables MA RA until we return,' replied one the sages and as they left, the robber fell to the ground and began to recite the syllables; although he did not realize it, he was reciting the name RAMA.

The robber squatted for years repeating the chant. He sat so still that an ant hill began to form around him. But the robber still did not move and finally he was completely covered by it. The years passed and the robber sat motionless in his ant hill, still chanting the name of RAMA, until one day, the holy men decided to return. As they approached, the ant hill burst open and the robber stood up. His hair and his beard were long and matted and he glowed with an aura of holiness. He seemed altogether a new man. Since he had repented his sins and been born anew from the womb of an ant hill, the sages named him Valmiki (from *valmik*: the Sanskrit word for ant hill).

Valmiki's years of meditation left him with enormous spiritual power and holy men came from far and near to see him. One day he decided to visit the River Tamasa which rose in the Rhiksha mountains, and to bathe in its holy waters at the spot where it joined the Ganges. On the way his attention was caught by two doves billing and cooing, and he remarked to his disciples how innocent the love of animals was. Hardly had he finished speaking when an arrow appeared as if from nowhere and pierced the heart of one of the doves. Valmiki groaned at the sight and cursed the hunter. When he had finished his curse, Valmiki realized that his words contained a certain rhythm. Valmiki's curse is said by some to be the first poetic stanza ever written. Because it was the result of the grief of the first poet, he called that type of verse 'shloka' after the Hindu word for grief, which is *shoka*.

Later the same day, Brahma himself visited Valmiki.

'All that you have experienced was part of my plan. Now I instruct you to write the story of Ram.'

'But I do not know the story of Ram,' Valmiki protested.

'Write everything you know and even that which you do not know. Your story will live as long as the oceans and mountains exist,' replied Brahma.

Then he left. Valmiki was deeply concerned, but he decided to put all his faith in Brahma and to try to fulfil his divine command. He fell into a deep trance, concentrating on nothing but Rama or Ram, the man whose name he had repeated for so many years. Then a miracle happened. Before Valmiki's eyes there appeared the great city of Ayodhya and as he watched, the life of Ram unfolded.

This is how the great epic the *Ramayan* came to be written. It is said that those who read it with respect and concentration have all their sins washed away.

Ram's early life

The beautiful city of Ayodhya was the capital of the kingdom of Kosala, and was ruled by Dasharat who was known far and wide for his bravery in battle. He had even occasionally helped the gods in their fights against demons—a privilege that was granted to few mortals. Dasharat's people loved him just as the gods did, because he was kind and fair, but Dasharat had a deep sadness in him for in spite of marrying three times he had no heir. His wives, princesses from important kingdoms, all remained childless. One day, Vasishta the court sage advised Dasharat to perform a sacrifice in order to obtain a son.

A sacrificial fire was lit and Vasishta began performing the ceremonial rituals. As he prayed, the flames leaped high into the air and a human form emerged from the fire. Nobody realized that it was Vishnu the Restorer. 'Give this to your three queens,' Vishnu said to Dasharat and handed him a bowl full of nectar, 'and they will bear you sons.' Dasharat fell to his knees and thanked the god and rushed to give the precious food to his wives. Not long afterwards Kaushaliya, his first queen, gave birth to a son who was named Rama-Chandra. The second queen, Kaikeyi, gave birth to Bharat; and Sumitra, the youngest queen, gave birth to the twins Lakshman and Shatrughan.

As the boys grew, Rama-chandra proved himself highly skilled in the ways of kings and was equally adept in the skills of the warrior. He resembled the supreme spirit Vishnu, for Vishnu had indeed been partly reborn in him for a special purpose on Earth. However, even Ram did not realize that part of him was a god. Ram was as dark as a rain cloud. His eyes were shaped like the lotus-flower and glistened as blackly as his curly hair. Although his frame was slight and slim, he had the powerful waist and chest of a lion. His arms were remarkably long and very powerful and his hands, though strong, had delicate fingers tipped with nails which glittered like mother-of-pearl. And his face glowed like the clear autumn moon, with the beauty of truth and love. Everyone loved him and it was obvious he would be a most suitable king. Dasharat, however, had promised his second wife's father when he sought her hand that her son would be the crown prince of Ayodhya. This wife, Kaikeyi, was Dasharat's favourite wife and he could not bear to upset her. Fortunately, Kaikeyi agreed wholeheartedly that Ram should be king.

From the beginning, Lakshman was especially deeply attached to his brother Ram as was his twin brother Shatrughan to Bharat, but all four princes loved each other deeply and grew up happily together learning arts, sciences, scriptures and statecraft from Vasishta. One day while they were still young boys, the great sage Vishvamitra arrived in Dasharat's court.
'I need the help of Ram,' he demanded, 'to slay a demoness who is attacking me.'
'He is only a child,' protested the king, but Vasishta advised him to let Ram go with Vishvamitra.
'He is one of the world's great sages,' he counselled. 'It will be beneficial for Ram to spend some time with him.'

Unwillingly Dasharat gave in to the pressure put upon him and Ram and his brother Lakshman went back with Vishvamitra to his hermitage. When they arrived there, Vishvamitra gave Ram magical weapons and after a bitter fight Ram vanquished the demoness.
'Now,' said the sage, 'you will travel with me to the capital of Vaideha, where King Janak is choosing a husband for his daughter Sita.'

This had been the real reason why Vishvamitra had wanted Ram to leave the court with him for he had known that Ram would soon defeat the demoness.

Sita was the daughter of the Earth. While she was a baby, she had appeared to King Janak from a furrow in a ploughed field, and had been brought up as his daughter. Sita was in fact another incarnation of Lakshmi, the eternal wife of Vishnu in all his incarnations; this time she had been reborn to marry Ram. She always left a train of light in her wake as a mark of her divine origin. She was as delicate and graceful as a swan: her raven black hair was threaded with pearls. Her forehead was like a half-moon, golden and glittering with the jewelled ornaments she wore. Her eyebrows were arched perfectly like a bow and below them glowed fawn-like eyes shaded with glistening lashes. Her lips glowed soft as corals, her neck was slender and dimpled. Her voice was as sweet as the nightingale's song. Everyone who saw Sita loved her instantly.

All Sita's suitors had to enter a contest known as a swayamvara to decide the one who should marry her. A bow of Shiv had been placed the centre of the court and the one who was able to lift it would be her husband. Hundreds tried and failed. Then, to Sita's great joy, Ram not only lifted the bow, but was strong enough to break it as well. News of Ram's forthcoming wedding was sent to Ayodhya. King Dasharat was overjoyed at the news and arrived for the celebrations. After the festivities were over, Ram, Sita and Dasharat returned home where all Ayodhya waited to greet them and more feasting and merriment took place to welcome Sita. Finally, a brother of Queen Kaikeyi spoke to Dasharat.
'My father wishes his grandson Bharat to return with me to live in our kingdom for several years and learn about our customs. Now that the festivities are over, Your Majesty, may I take Bharat home with me?'
Reluctantly Dasharat agreed and Bharat left for his grandfather's court.

The years went by and Ram proved to be a kind husband. Sita was a devoted wife and the two were deeply in love. Dasharat missed Bharat and longed to see him, yet one matter worried him constantly: Ram must be declared king before Bharat's return, because Dasharat wanted to avoid any arguments about which brother should become the new king. The elderly king called a council of ministers, sages and allied kings and announced his decision to crown Ram, King of Ayodhya.

The council discussed the matter and unanimously approved his choice. Ram was called before the assembly and Dasharat officially acknowledged him heir-apparent. Still anxious, the king summoned Ram to his personal chambers that night and told Ram he would crown him the very next day. Ram was stunned that his father was considering holding

the coronation before Bharat could return for it. 'Such affairs have the power to create treacherous impulses in the most faithful of men so it is best to do this quickly,' the king said, brushing aside Ram's protests and Ram was dismissed to fast along with Sita in preparation for the next day's ceremony.

The king ordered his ministers to make all the necessary arrangements for the coronation, and went to Kaikeyi's rooms to give her the news. 'Your queen is in the Chamber of Protest, my liege,' said Kaikeyi's servant.
The Chamber of Protest was reserved for any queen with a complaint and had never been used during Dasharat's reign. He made his way there anxiously.

Kaikeyi lay sprawled on the floor of her chamber, her hair dishevelled, her jewels scattered across the floor, and she was weeping and lamenting. Dasharat fell to his knees and stroked her hair gently, asking, 'Who has upset you, my beloved queen?'
'No-one,' she replied, 'but I ask you for the two wishes you promised when I saved you on the battlefield. If you choose not to grant them, I shall kill myself.'

Dasharat remained silent a moment as that battle flashed through his mind. The god Indra had asked Dasharat to fight the demon Shambar who was plaguing the gods. Dasharat had defeated the demon armies but was left lying severely wounded on the battlefield with little chance of living. Kaikeyi, who had insisted on accompanying him to battle, had him carried to her tent and nursed him night and day until he recovered. The king had been so grateful he had promised to grant Kaikeyi two wishes.
'You are alive, my lord,' Kaikeyi had replied, 'I need nothing else. Let me save my wishes and ask for them when I need them.'
'You and Ram are dearer to me than anything else in the world,' the king now said, realizing that Kaikeyi was about to ask him for something he would find painful to grant. 'I swear that I shall do what you want.'
'Then first I wish you to send Ram into exile for fourteen years and second I wish you to proclaim Bharat king,' Kaikeyi said swiftly.

Dasharat was broken-hearted. He could not believe that Kaikeyi, who had always said she loved Ram more than her own son and had often suggested he should be king, had now changed her mind completely. He argued with Kaikeyi throughout the night, but Kaikeyi's mind was made up and Dasharat knew he must keep his promise to Kaikeyi and her father.

When morning came, the king was utterly worn down. He was distressed by the idea of losing his beloved son in his own old age, and could not bring himself to speak to Ram when the young prince came to get his blessing before the coronation.

Ram was concerned, 'Have I upset my father?' he wondered, then looking at Kaikeyi's harsh expression, he asked.
'Have I displeased the king? Tell me mother, why does my father looks so dejected?'
'Then listen, Ram,' replied Kaikeyi sternly. 'Your father loves you more than even his honour so he hesitates to command you to go into exile for fourteen years, while Bharat is crowned and established king of Ayodhya.'
'Thank you for telling me mother,' Ram said. 'There is no greater virtue than to obey one's parents. I will leave immediately. Bharat will make an able king.'

Ram sadly said farewell to his heartbroken father and then went to Queen Kaushaliya, his real mother, to say goodbye to her. He explained how the decision had come about and begged her to be kind to Dasharat who was deeply unhappy at Ram's exile. Although grief-stricken, Kaushaliya agreed with Ram, praying for his happiness in exile.

Then Ram went to say goodbye to Sita and to comfort her but Sita refused to be separated from her husband.
'If you can to live in hardship away from home and your beloved family,' she said, 'then I will go with you. How can I be happy living in luxury without you?'

His brother Lakshman also refused to stay behind and that very day they left the kingdom. Ram led the way, dressed like a holy man, with tangled hair and a leopard skin to cover his body. The only sign that he was a warrior was the quiver of arrows which hung from his shoulder and his precious bow.

Ram and the demons

The three left the city of Ayodhya and made their way across the River Ganges and up into the mountains and forests of the Himalayas where they lived a holy life, filled with fasting and prayer.

The months passed and one day Ram was meditating when he sensed a disturbance in the forest. The birds were flying from the trees and animals were scurrying away to hide in the undergrowth. Lakshman climbed to the top of a tall tree to see what was causing the turmoil. 'It is Bharat,' he shouted down to Ram. 'He is coming with an army of men. No doubt he wants to make his throne more secure by killing us.'

Ram shook his head wisely. 'Bharat is a good man,' he replied. 'It is because he loves us that he has made the journey. He probably wants us to come back to Ayodhya.'

Ram's words calmed his quick-tempered brother. When Bharat arrived he greeted his brothers with affection. Then he said, 'You should be in Ayodhya, Ram. Our father has died of grief and our country needs its true king. You should be on the throne, ruling the kingdom. Let me remain here to serve out your exile for you while you return to Ayodhya.'

Ram hugged his brother and said gently. 'Our father gave his word to Kaikeyi that her wishes would be fulfilled. It is our duty to ensure his word is kept.'

Bharat and the wise man Vasishta who had accompanied him pleaded with Ram to change his mind, but Ram was determined to obey his father's instructions as well as he could. Realizing this, Bharat held out a pair of golden slippers he had brought with him.

'Put your feet into these a moment,' he told Ram and when Ram had done so, Bharat picked up the slippers reverently.

'I will place these slippers by your throne as a token that it is really yours,' he said, 'and I will rule the kingdom in your name until you return. But if you do not return in fourteen years, I will burn myself on a funeral pyre.' Then he left his brothers and returned to Ayodhya.

After Bharat had left, Ram decided to move on. The three travelled deeper into the forest and soon met some hermits.

'We are constantly plagued by the demons and other monsters which infest this forest,' said the holy men. 'They kill several of us each day, just for sport. We know you are Ram the mighty warrior. We want you to give us your word that you will protect us from these fearsome monsters.'

Ram promised to defend the holy men and the three continued their journey into the forest until they met a wise man named Sutikshin. 'I can see that you will have many demons to fight in the future,' Sutikshin told them, 'and you will often be the conqueror. But beware of a gazelle who plays in a forest glade for it is a sign of ill fortune.'

None of them understood his mysterious words, but they thanked him and set off again on their journey. After a time they arrived at a lake where they heard exquisite voices singing, the voices of five heavenly maidens who had once descended there from heaven. Ram decided to build a home with Sita and Lakshman on the shores of the beautiful lake. For ten years they lived there and Ram continued to keep his promise to protect the holy men from the monsters and demons of the forest. He did it so well that eventually there were no more monsters.

Ram and his companions decided to set out on their travels. On their way, they met an enormous vulture who introduced himself as Jatayu, the king of birds.

'I was a friend of your dead father,' Jatayu said, 'and I want you to consider me your friend as well.'

Ram thanked Jatayu and the three continued on their way until they arrived at a place called Panchavati where they decided to stay. But they were not destined to remain there long. A demoness named Shurpanakha saw Ram one day and fell in love with him. She transformed herself into a beautiful young woman and went to Ram.

'Become my husband,' she said to him. 'I will eat Sita and we can roam the forests happily together.'

Ram could not be tempted. 'I love my wife dearly. You must look elsewhere for a husband.'

Slighted, Shurpanakha tried to kill Sita, but Lakshman cut off her ears and nose and chased her into the forest.

Disfigured and longing for revenge, Shurpanakha went to Janastan, the land of demons, ruled by her brother Khar.

'Look at your sister's plight,' she roared in humiliation. 'You must avenge me with your hordes of demons. I thirst for the blood of Sita and Lakshman.'

'I will not rest until I have taken revenge,' Khar promised. He assembled an army of 14,000 demons and set out for Panchavati.

The noise of the approaching army was so loud that the gods in their heavens heard it and looked down to see what was happening. When Ram saw the army, he hid Sita and Lakshman in a cave and as the demons came nearer, he shot a stream of arrows from his mighty bow. Soon

only Khar was left alive. With a strength born from despair, Khar pulled the bow out of Ram's grasp and shattered Ram's shield with his club. Then he uprooted a huge tree and hurled it at Ram, who leaped out of its path just in time. Ram swiftly picked up the bow and again showered Khar with a volley of arrows. Finally Khar, the last of the demon army, was also killed and the realm of the demons was utterly desolated.

In Heaven the gods heaved a sigh of relief. The mission for which Ram had been put on Earth was soon to be accomplished.

Sita and the demon king

The kingdom of Lanka had been created for Kuvera, the god of wealth, and even its humblest buildings were made from solid gold: it was filled with splendid gardens and white cloud-like mansions. Vishvakarma, the gods' architect, had originally suspended it in mid-air, but it now lay in the middle of the Indian Ocean where it had been flung by Vayu, the wind god, in a moment of fury. It is still there today and is known as the island of Sri Lanka.

The capital of Lanka was protected by seven broad moats and seven enormous walls of stone and metal, but Kuvera no longer ruled there because many years before, the demon Ravan had defeated him and taken the kingdom of Lanka from him.

Ravan was the brother of the demons Shurpanakha and Khar and was the creature most hated by the gods. His mother was a demoness but his father was a Brahmin who had shown him how to pray and fast. He had prayed and fasted so devotedly that the god Brahma was compelled to grant him a special wish in payment. Ravan had wished to be made invulnerable to attack by any god or demon.

Ravan was terrifying to look at, for he had twenty arms and ten heads. His teeth shone pale gold like the light of a crescent moon. His mountainous body was covered with the ugly scars of a million battles with gods and demons. Ravan could split open mountains, stir up the

seas and tear the sun and moon from the sky. Since no god could hurt him, Ravan humiliated the gods by forcing them to do menial tasks in his palace. Vayu the wind god swept the floors for him; Kuvera the god of wealth supplied him with gold; Varuna the sea god brought him water and Agni the fire god was his cook. Ravan was rapidly becoming the most powerful of all creatures until Vishnu found a solution.

When Ravan had forced Brahma to grant him his wish, he had asked only for protection against the gods and demons; he had been too arrogant to feel threatened by mere men and animals. This gave Vishnu an idea. He himself would be reborn to King Dasharat in his seventh incarnation as his eldest son, Rama-chandra, and as a man he would bring about the downfall of this all-powerful demon. He would not, however, be able to remember his previous existence as a god and would have to rely upon his human ability and courage alone. So, while Ram acted out his destiny, the gods bided their time, secure in the knowledge that one day they would be free of Ravan. Meanwhile, Ravan lived in luxury in the beautiful kingdom of Lanka.

One day, Ravan was sitting in his court with his many wives when he heard the sounds of hysterical bellows and Shurpanakha burst into the room.

'Your sister thirsts for revenge,' the demoness howled, rolling her hideous eyes. 'Our brother Khar and all of his demons have been destroyed by Ram of Kosala and he must be punished. I will personally suck the blood of Lakshman who has lopped off my nose and ears, and the blood of Sita who is the cause of my trouble. Ram's beauty attracted me and I turned myself into a beautiful woman to tempt him. I thought that no man could resist me, but I could not overcome Ram's love for Sita. She is more virtuous and lovely than any woman ever known.' Bitterly, Shurpanakha described Sita's beauty.

Ravan immediately desired Sita for himself and decided to seize her at once. He summoned his magic chariot and flew across the ocean to the place where a demon named Marich lived. 'You must help me destroy this Ram and obtain his wife Sita for me,' Ravan commanded, 'for Ram has killed 14,000 demons and disfigured my sister without provocation.'
'You do not know Ram,' replied Marich, 'he is perfection personified and commands all the forces of good. You cannot defeat him.'
'Not even the gods with their combined powers can stop me,' thundered Ravan. 'You have forgotten my power, how dare you contradict me! It is your place to obey. Now do as I say or I will kill you.'

He gave Marich careful instructions and took him to Panchavati where Ram and his wife and brother were living. There Marich transformed himself into a golden deer and began to graze peacefully in the clearing by Ram's home. Sita caught sight of the deer as she walked among the flowers. It looked at her with melting, sad eyes and she became enchanted by it.

'Ram, Lakshman,' she called. 'Come and look at this deer. Catch it and bring it to me so that I will always be able to look at it.'

Ram remembered the warning that a gazelle would be an ill omen but Sita would not be convinced. Lakshman also tried to reason with her, explaining that the gazelle might be one of the few demons left, but Sita did not believe there was any danger and finally Ram agreed to catch the deer for her. However, he told Lakshman not to leave Sita's side and drew a circle around her.

'This magic circle will protect you from demons. Do not step out of it until I return with the deer,' he warned and left to try and catch the lovely animal. The chase was long but at last Ram was close enough to take aim. He intended only to wound the animal slightly so that he could catch it but he misfired and his arrow sank deep into the deer's body. As it fell to the earth, it cried out in Ram's voice, 'Ah, Lakshman! Alas, my Sita!' Sita heard her husband's voice in the distance and thought that he must be hurt and in need of help.

'Go to him immediately,' Sita told Lakshman, 'Ram needs you.'

Lakshman protested. 'Ram left me here to protect you,' he replied. 'He does not need my help.' But Sita wept and pleaded until he agreed to see if Ram had indeed been wounded.

No sooner had Lakshman disappeared into the forest than a holy man passed by. 'Who are you who live in the forest, yet are dressed in silk like one of noble birth?' he asked. 'Do you have no protector?'

'I am Sita,' she replied, greeting the holy man respectfully, 'I live here with my husband Ram and his brother Lakshman.'

'Then do your duty, virtuous Sita,' said the holy man, 'and provide me with some food.'

Sita stepped out of the magic circle to fetch food for the holy man and as soon as she had done so, he seized her.

'I am the ten-headed Ravan, ruler of Lanka,' he announced. 'Become my bride—you shall command him who commands the gods.'

Sita resisted, struggling and pleading, but Ravan gripped her firmly by her hair and, fastening her to his chariot, he flew with her through the air. As the chariot made its way to Lanka, Sita caught sight of the vulture Jatayu. 'King of birds,' she begged, 'tell Ram that Ravan has kidnapped me.'

Jatayu swooped in front of the chariot, spreading his massive wings to bar Ravan's progress, but the demon drew his sword and sliced off one of the bird's wings so that he tumbled bleeding to the ground, calling to Sita. 'I cannot help you, Sita, but I will tell Ram of your plight.'

As the chariot flew on, Sita threw her jewellery to the ground, hoping to create a trail for Ram to follow. As they passed over a mountain peak far below, she saw a group of powerful monkeys and threw down to them some jewellery and a scarf made from cloth of gold in the hope that if Ram came that way in his search, the monkeys would show them to him.

All too soon, they arrived at Lanka where Ravan installed Sita in his palace and started to court her in the hope that she would agree to be his bride. Sita however had no intention of giving in to Ravan. She veiled her face and reminded him repeatedly that she was the wife of Ram and that she would never agree to marry him even if the penalty was death. Finally, Ravan grew weary of her resistance and threw her into a grove of ashoka trees where she was guarded by female demons.

'If you do not come to your senses within a year, I shall eat you,' he told her.

Sita waited desperately for Ram to come and save her, but many months passed. Her clothes grew tattered and dirty, her hair lost its shine, and her already slender body wasted away until she was scarcely more than skin and bone. Still Ram did not come.

Yet the gods rejoiced, because they knew that the day would soon come when Ram would attack Lanka to rescue Sita and when that day arrived, Ravan would meet his fate.

Ram's search for Sita

Ram was not surprised to find that the golden deer had turned into a demon as it died but he was immediately worried about Sita's safety and ran back home. On the way he met Lakshman. 'Why have you left Sita alone?' he demanded angrily.

'We heard your voice and thought you were in danger,' Lakshman explained, 'Sita insisted that I should see why you called.' Suspecting the worst, the two brothers hurried home. On the way they saw Jatayu the vulture lying in a pool of blood.

'Ram,' whispered Jatayu. 'Make haste. Ravan, the demon-king of Lanka, has abducted Sita. I could not save her, though I tried. But I am not sad for I can see golden forests and fields and I know I am about to die and go to heaven. Ravan went southwards. Follow him. Do not despair, you will find Sita.'

Jatayu died and a chariot of fire swooped down and carried his spirit away and out of the flames of the funeral pyre which Ram and Lakshman had lit for him.

The brothers travelled southwards, searching for information about Sita. Soon they entered a terrifying forest which was filled with monsters and wild beasts. Suddenly they saw the trees before them being ripped out of the soil and crushed underfoot. A huge ogre with arms the size of tree trunks was striding towards them, tearing up everything that stood in his way. The most terrifying thing about him was that he had no head.

Ram and Lakshman had heard stories of this ogre and knew that his name was Kabandha. Lakshman trembled with fear for the first time in his life, and even Ram was not sure that they could defeat this creature, but the brothers did not intend to give up without a struggle. They ducked beneath his flailing arms and attacking at the same time, cut them off with their swords. With his arms severed Kabandha lay wounded and helpless. Then in a gentle voice that seemed to come out of the air, he asked who had destroyed him. When he found they were Ram and Lakshman, he exclaimed joyfully, 'I am released at last!'

Kabandha then explained that he was an immortal who had tried to challenge Indra's power. The angry god had cut off his head and told him that he would remain headless until Ram and Lakshman cut off his arms. 'Although I am immortal, I now choose to die and I ask you to cremate my body with all the proper ceremonies so that my soul may find release,' he told them. 'In return I shall tell you how you might find Sita.'

Ram did as Kabandha asked and as the flames rose higher, a radiant being emerged from the fire and spoke to them.

'Go and find Sugriv, the exiled monkey-king. His brother Valin has usurped his throne and you must help Sugriv to regain it. Sugriv and his monkeys will then help you rescue Sita for these monkeys are of divine origin and have superhuman powers. Sugriv's father is said to be Surya the Sun.'

Encouraged, Ram and Lakshman hurried on southward. Soon they arrived at a lake which was ablaze with the dazzling colour and beauty of lotuses and lilies.

Ram waded across the lake, heavy-hearted with longing for Sita and as he strode across, he saw a powerful monkey who was as tall as a tower. The monkey's face blazed as red as a ruby and his body glowed like molten gold. His tail stretched out to an enormous distance and he stood on a lofty rock roaring like thunder. As he saw the princes approach, he leaped agilely from the rock and flew over to them, speaking in a voice which was gentle and respectful.

'Know that I am Hanuman, son of Vayu the god of the wind. My master is Sugriv the monkey king, who has lost his kingdom and his wife to his brother. We heard that you were nearby and know your reputations as warriors. Sugriv has sent me to greet you and offer his friendship.'

When Hanuman heard that the brothers had come to seek help, he asked them to sit on his shoulders and with one mighty leap he carried them to the mountain where Sugriv was. Sugriv showed them the scarf and jewellery that Sita had flung down from Ravan's flying chariot. 'Help me win back my kingdom from my

wicked brother Valin,' said Sugriv, 'and I promise to help you bring back Sita.'

'We gladly agree to help you,' Ram promised.

The next day Ram and Lakshman set out with Sugriv, Hanuman and their small band of monkeys. They hid themselves in the trees around Valin's city while Sugriv went forward to stand at its gates and bellow terrifyingly to Valin to come out. Infuriated by the challenge, Valin led his soldiers out for battle. The brothers fought angrily in single hand-to-hand combat until Sugriv had to signal for Ram's help. When Ram saw that his friend was weakening, he aimed his arrow at Valin's heart and killed Valin instantly.

Ram had fulfilled his promise. Sugriv was king once again and was ready to help to find Sita. But the summer monsoons had come and the heavy rains made further searching impossible. Ram had to wait for the summer's end before the search for Sita could begin again.

The adventures of Hanuman

When the monsoon rain ended at last, it was time for Sugriv to pay his debt to Ram. Sugriv called Hanuman to him. Hanuman could fly and leap so high that he could seize the clouds. He was also a great magician and so knowledgeable that he could interpret the shastras, the Hindu books of wisdom, better than anyone else. If anyone could find Sita, Hanuman could.

'In one month,' commanded Sugriv, 'you must report back with what you have found.'

Ram had no doubt that Hanuman would find his beloved Sita.

'As a token of my faith in you, Hanuman,' he said, 'here is my ring. When you see Sita, show it to her and she will know that you have come from me.'

Hanuman set off with an army of monkeys, and Jambavan the king of the bears and his army went too. Thousands of monkeys and bears searched every corner of the land but without success. As the thirtieth day drew near, Hanuman was in despair, humiliated by his failure to find Sita. He called his army of searchers and made an announcement.

'I have failed in my mission and wasted a month. I cannot face the humiliation of my failure and deserve to die.'

Hanuman was about to kill himself when one of his companions noticed a weak-looking vulture hovering above in the hope that he might make a meal of the dead monkey. The monkey waved to the bird and shouted, 'Your king Jatayu saw the wife of Ram being carried away. Can you direct us to her?'

The vulture realized these were superhuman creatures on a virtuous quest: he decided to help them.

'I am Sampati, brother of Jatayu,' he said. 'My wings were burned once when I flew too close to Surya the Sun god. I have lost my strength so I cannot help you physically, but I did once hear a woman calling to Ram and Lakshman as Ravan's chariot flew overhead. I know that the demon lives on an island city a hundred leagues over the southern ocean. It was built by Vishvakarma and is called Lanka.'

Surya the Sun god had promised Sampati that his wings would grow strong again if he ever helped Ram and the bird was still speaking when he found his strength returning and his feathers growing back. The bears and monkeys thanked him for his help and as the bird began to try his newly regained power, they sped off to the shores of the Indian Ocean. When they arrived, Hanuman breathed in deeply, swelling his chest with the sea winds. He brandished his tail, and thundered up a nearby mountain with a joyous but terrifying roar. At the top of the mountain, Hanuman paused and prayed, preparing for the mighty leap which would bring him to Lanka, alone, enormous and magnificent. None of his companions would be able to follow him.

Then Hanuman leaped into the air like an arrow, flying among the clouds and over the waves far below until he landed on the island of Lanka. When at last he reached its capital, he decided to wait until dark and then crawl through the gates, but the city's demon sentries noticed him and attacked him. Hanuman slew them all in the combat which followed.

Victorious, Hanuman marched into Ravan's palace and searched every terrace and room until he was certain that Sita was not there.

He was walking through the courtyards on his way out when he saw a light glittering through the leaves of some ashoka trees. He sprang towards them and saw that the light was coming from Sita who still glowed with a pale radiance. Weak from distress and hunger, Ram's wife sat as still as a statue in her grief. As Hanuman wondered what to do next, he heard a fanfare of trumpets and Ravan arrived. As always Ravan spoke to Sita of his love and told her she was foolish to pine for Ram, when he, whom even the gods feared, was offering to marry her. But Sita refused to listen, and instead drew a line in the ground between them. 'I will never step across this line, because I am Ram's wife and love only him. You should not look at the wife of another man. Even now, if you return me to Ram, he might forgive you,' she said. Furiously, Ravan turned away. 'I have waited nearly a full year for you,' he bellowed. 'If you have not changed your mind in two months when the year is complete, I will have you slaughtered for my breakfast.' Then he marched out.

Hanuman dropped lithely to the floor as soon as Ravan had left. Head bowed, he approached Sita and respectfully showed her the ring which Ram had sent. He introduced himself, telling her, 'Ram told me to find you. He is well and worries constantly about you.'

Sita asked tenderly about Ram and Lakshman and inquired why they had not yet come to rescue her. Gently, Hanuman explained how difficult it had been to find her. 'Tell Ram from me,' she said when she had heard the whole story, 'that I will live for one month more. After that I swear that I shall die.' Saying this she handed Hanuman a jewel so that he could prove he had seen her.

Hanuman promised faithfully to do as Sita said and flew off, intending to wreak as much havoc and ruin in Lanka as he could before finally returning to Ram with his news. He began by destroying the demonesses who guarded Sita. When Ravan's terrified courtiers told him that a fearsome monkey had ripped apart the ashoka grove, Ravan sent 80,000 servants to stop him but Hanuman found a club and crushed their skulls with one powerful swing. Then he set Ravan's temple alight and destroyed many of Ravan's ministers and warriors. Finally, Ravan's mightiest son, Indrajit, shot an arrow which had been given to Ravan by Brahma himself and which had a spark of divine power. The arrow struck Hanuman down and while he lay helpless he was brought to Ravan. Hanuman spoke proudly even in captivity.

'I am Hanuman, the son of Vayu and messenger of Ram. I have had to fight my way into your presence to deliver Ram's message. Return Sita to her true husband. This is Ram's order and if you do not obey it you will be destroyed.'

Ravan was so enraged by Hanuman's words that he wanted to have him killed on the spot but his ministers had another idea. 'It is unwise to kill the messenger of an enemy,' they advised. 'Why not give Ram an idea of our power instead by setting Hanuman's tail alight? A monkey's tail is most important to him after all, and without it he will be as deformed as your unlucky sister Shurpanakha.'

Ravan roared with approval at the suggestion, so the demons greased Hanuman's tail and wrapped it with pieces of cottonwool to make it burn easily. Hanuman's tail was set alight but although the flames blazed fiercely, the fire god Agni protected Hanuman and he did not feel their heat. As he prepared to leave Lanka, Hanuman decided to make one last attempt to disorganize the island before the war began. He made a mighty leap onto Ravan's fortress where he lashed his enormous, curved tail so that fire rained down on the terraces and courtyards until the whole city was one massive flame. Then, thanking Agni for his aid and offering the burning city to him as a sacrifice, he ran to the beaches and plunged his tail into the ocean to put out the fire. With another mighty leap he returned to the mountain on the mainland where he was given a hero's welcome and proudly told the monkeys and the bears about his adventures. Then they set out on the journey back to Ram, who was waiting impatiently for news of Sita.

The death of Ravan

Hanuman gave Sita's jewel to Ram and told him everything that had happened while he had been away. Ram immediately set out with the monkeys and the bears for the southernmost shores of India. Soon after they arrived, a figure approached Ram and identified himself.

'I am Vibhishan, the brother of Ravan,' he said. 'I have tried to persuade Ravan to return Sita to you and stop the bloodshed, but he will not listen to reason so I have come to help Ram in any way I can. I have a special power; I can see Indrajit, Ravan's warrior son, wherever he may be. That may prove helpful to Ram in the fight which lies ahead.'

Rama thanked Vibhishan and swore to protect him since he had left his home and family to help him. Then Ram made his way down to the shore to pray for the help of Sagar, the god of the ocean, in crossing over to Lanka.

On Sagar's advice, the monkeys built a bridge to cross the hundred leagues of ocean between India and Lanka and soon Ram, Lakshman and the armies of bears and monkeys had arrived on the island. The monkeys quickly spread out along the beaches, taking up guard and shouting excitedly. Ram then sent a message to Ravan. 'I have arrived on Lanka. Return my wife or I shall destroy you and your demons with my arrows. If you do not obey my warning, you will lose everything.'

Ravan was infuriated by Ram's arrogant message and ordered his mighty son Indrajit to march out against him. The battle raged fiercely, but Ram's forces were doing well until Indrajit made himself invisible and shot Ram and Lakshman with his magic arrow. It was the same arrow that had struck down Hanuman, for it always returned to its owner after it had been used and it never missed its target. The arrow injured both of the brothers severely and Indrajit then began shooting at the others—many monkeys and bears were wounded by his arrows for they could not see where the next attack would come from.

At last Ravan's brother Vibhishan used his own special powers to find Indrajit and wound him: Indrajit was forced to withdraw, boasting that he had killed Ram and Lakshman. The surviving bears and monkeys gazed mournfully down at Ram's unconscious body and to their relief, saw him stir. Suddenly there was a great flash of fire in the sky. Out of it emerged a magnificent eagle: it was Vishnu's mount, Garuda. Swooping down like a fiery meteor he spoke to Ram, 'I have been sent to restore you and Lakshman back to health.' He then embraced them both, filling them with new life, and flew back into the sky.

In his palace, Ravan heard the excited cheers of the monkeys and rallied the best of his warriors. Fearsome demons charged out of the city but Hanuman killed them all single-handedly, and Ravan and his soldiers were driven back. Ravan knew his only chance now was to awaken his brother, the gluttonous giant Kumbhakarna who slept for six months of the year. It took the noise of everyone in the city to wake him but after much persuasion, Kumbhakarna agreed to help Ravan and gulped down 2000 jars of liquor to strengthen himself before setting out to kill Ram. Kumbhakarna drunkenly lurched towards Ram's armies whirling his mace around his head. The battle seemed lost and once more the bears and monkeys were slaughtered in their hundreds. Ram once again set his bow to work, aiming a steady stream of arrows at the giant. At last, Kumbhakarna fell to the ground but he still waved his arms and legs about and knocked down whole troops of monkeys before Ram raised his bow and killed him with a deadly arrow. For a time, the fighting ceased but soon Indrajit had recovered enough to return to the battle. He flew in his chariot above the ranks of bears and monkeys, showering them with arrows and lances. Only when Jambavan, Sugriv, Ram and Lakshman had all been wounded did Indrajit withdraw to his palace and the battle ended for the day.

That night, Jambavan the king of the bears told Hanuman of some healing herbs on Mount Kailash, the home of Shiv.
'The herbs will heal our wounded,' he said, 'if you can find them.' Hanuman flew directly to Kailash but was unable to recognize the herbs. Desperate to return before dawn, he tore off the

whole top of the mountain and brought it to Jambavan, who selected the right herbs and cured the injured. Then Hanuman put the summit back in its original place.

Filled with new strength and enthusiasm, the monkeys were now determined to end this bitter war swiftly. King Sugriv led them in a charge onto the battlements of Ravan's fortress and set the city ablaze. In the following battle, they killed all the remaining demon warriors except Indrajit and Ravan himself. With all his warriors dead, the ten-headed king turned to his son.

'Ram is mighty, but you have proved yourself to be mightier, because you have already wounded him twice. Kill Ram and Lakshman and we can still win this war.'

Indrajit attacked again, using every demonic trick he knew to weaken Ram and Lakshman. In order to dishearten Ram, he conjured up an image of Sita in his carriage, an image which

looked as if she had been beheaded. Then he again attacked from the sky, but finally Lakshman notched an arrow which had been given to him by Indra and shot it at Indrajit. The arrow ripped the demon's head from his shoulders and the demon was defeated at last.

Now there was nothing left for Ravan but to fight Ram himself. Heavy-hearted at the loss of his favourite son, Ravan charged out of his fortress in his magic chariot. He flew into the air and began to shoot arrows down at Ram with all his twenty arms. The gods considered this was unfair and they sent Matali the heavenly charioteer to raise him up to an equal height. Then Ram chanted a hymn to the gods and drinking three sips of water purified himself and continued the fight with Ravan. Finally, his arrow pierced Ravan's heart and knocked him out of his chariot and onto the ground.

Ravan's brother, Vibhishan, looked at the once powerful demon lying dead on the ground caked in blood and dust.

'If only you had done as I said,' he wept, 'all this destruction could have been avoided.'

Ram laid his hand on Vibhishan's shoulder, 'You are a hero. Heroes must fight to the death. It is not suitable for you to grieve in this manner. Now prepare to give your brother a proper funeral.'

Having buried Ravan with all the proper rites, Vibhishan was crowned king of Lanka in his place. After the ceremony, Ram sent Hanuman to give Sita the news of his victory.

Hanuman entered the ashoka grove with his head held high and his heart full of happiness. He bowed deeply before Sita, who was waiting anxiously for news of Rama.

'I bring you joyful news, my queen,' he said. 'Ram has asked me to tell you that the war is over, Ravan is dead and right has triumphed.' As he spoke, King Vibhishan's carriage approached in all its splendour. The newly crowned king alighted from the carriage and bowed before Sita.

'If it pleases you, the women of my family shall attend to you and prepare you to meet Ram again.'

Sita wept with joy when she knew Ram and Lakshman were safe and that she was about to be united with her husband. She was bathed in Vibhishan's palace, dressed in silks and adorned with jewels. Her hair was threaded with pearls and her skin perfumed with the most delicate and exotic fragrances. When she was ready, Vibhishan instructed his servants to bring out the most magnificent palanquin to carry her to Ram. It stopped by Ram and Sita stepped nimbly down, delighted to be reunited with her husband. She looked up at him shyly yet jubilantly but was stunned by his harsh expression.

'Daughter of Janak,' he said sternly, 'I have slain the enemy and rescued you. I have done my duty and satisfied the demands of honour. But I cannot take you back. You have been touched by Ravan. How can I know that you are pure? You are free to go where you choose, I have no desire for you.'

'If I was touched by Ravan,' replied Sita with spirit, 'it was not because I chose it. It seems I have waited a long time for a man who does not love me but fought a war merely to satisfy his honour. I married a valiant prince who defended the weak, but you speak now of mistrust and blame like a coarse commoner. You knew my plight when Hanuman told you where I was. Why did you not leave me to my resources? I have no reason to live if my character and my past devotion mean nothing to you.' She turned to Lakshman. 'Prepare a funeral pyre. I intend to enter the flames.'

Lakshman looked at Ram but Ram did not try to prevent him, so he did as Sita asked. When the pyre was ready, Sita walked three times around Ram, and prayed to the gods. As she entered the flames Sita whispered a prayer to Agni, god of fire.

'Protect me Agni for you know that I am pure of heart and body.'

Fearlessly Sita stood in the blazing flames awaiting her fate. As they watched, she was suddenly lifted up in the arms of Agni who appeared out of the flames and fixed his intense gaze on Ram.

'Ram,' he said. 'Your wife is chaste and sinless. Embrace her and return to Ayodhya to rule there with her at your side.'

As he spoke all the gods appeared before them. Last of all came Ram's dead father Dasharat in a flying chariot. He spoke gently to his son.

'Ram, you have played your part in a plan of the gods for they themselves could not destroy the demon Ravan. Sita's abduction and suffering were a part of the same plan. If she had not been abducted by Ravan, you would have had no reason to fight him.'

Dasharat turned to Sita. 'And you, Sita, must understand the pain and worry that lie behind Ram's words and continue to love and support him as you have always done.

When the king had finished speaking the god Shiv appeared, radiant with joy at the destruction of Ravan.

'You have now seen all the gods, Ram. This is a sign of your devoutness and valour. In return for your efforts, we wish to reward you. So ask for anything and it shall be yours.'

'Lord Shiv, I beg that you bring back to life all the monkeys and bears who have fought and died for me,' Ram said.

'It shall be done,' declared Shiv. 'The war dead will return from the shady kingdom of Yama.' As he spoke the monkeys and bears began to revive and bow down before the gods and Ram. Then Dasharat and the gods departed, commanding Ram to return immediately to Ayodhya. The magic chariot was prepared and it was not long before Ram was safely back in his kingdom with Sita and Lakshman.

As they entered the city, they met Bharat dressed in ragged clothes, his face saddened by his long separation from his brothers and the unwanted responsibility of ruling the kingdom. When he saw his brother, Bharat's expression changed to one of joy. He immediately bowed to the ground and put the gold sandals on Ram's feet. Ram embraced Bharat and blessed him and together they all returned to the palace. They were received by the court sage Vasishta who seated Ram and Sita on the jewelled throne and blessed them both.

Ram then invited all his valiant allies to his kingdom to thank them and reward them. His kingdom prospered during his reign, yielding rich harvests of grain and honey, and Ram ruled happily with Sita at his side.

The life of Krishna

When the god Vishnu was reborn on Earth for the eighth time, he came back as Krishna. Krishna does not simply possess a portion of Vishnu's character as do Ram and the other incarnations of Vishnu but is believed to be Vishnu himself in human form. It was Krishna who composed the great Indian religious book known as the *Bhagavad Gita* which speaks of humanity's role in the great pattern of the universe, and which tells us that if we are devoted to what is right and determined to fulfil our destiny we shall triumph over everything.

Krishna grew up to be a scholar, a philosopher and a great warrior, but he is most adored as the child-god who stole butter from the dairies and the romantic cowherd who won the hearts of all the local milkmaids with his flute-playing. The hymns sung across India both to the child and to the youth are so much a part of the daily lives of Hindus that they are used as lullabies and love songs. These very human aspects of Krishna's personality are the main reason for his immense popularity.

Krishna's story begins with the tyrannous rule of King Kans, who lived in the city of Mathura, between Agra and Delhi. He was the child of a sorcerer and his evil deeds brought great misery and devastation to the Earth which called out to the gods to destroy him. Vishnu decided that it was time to rid the world of this monstrous king. To accomplish it he would be reborn in Mathura as the eighth son of a nobleman named Vasudev and his wife Devika.

King Kans was suspicious and used his magic powers to discover that the eighth son of this couple was destined to kill him, yet he could not murder Vasudev and Devika in case this caused a rebellion of his subjects. Instead, Kans had the couple closely watched before the birth of each child and killed their first six sons as soon as they were born. Vasudev had another wife named Rohini who was so terrified by this hideous cruelty that she fled to the quiet village of Gokul in Vrindavan to seek refuge with the goat-herds. There Vishnu placed in her body Devika's seventh son who would also help in King Kans' destruction, and when he was born he was named Balaram. Vishnu told Devika and Vasudev what he had done and they told King Kans that Devika's baby had died.

Devika became pregnant again, and was placed under heavy guard as the time of the birth drew near. She gave birth to a baby boy but the couple's joy was short-lived when they remembered that he, too, was destined to die. As they gazed at the baby, desperately praying for his life, his appearance was transformed into that of the great god Vishnu and they realized that their baby son Krishna was Vishnu himself, re-incarnated.

'Do not be afraid,' Vishnu said. 'Carry me to the village of Gokul where Yashodha, the wife of the cowherd Nand is about to give birth to a baby girl. Bring her daughter back for Kans to see. Since he bears no ill-will to your girl children your troubles will be at an end.'

Vasudev looked helplessly at the heavily guarded and locked chamber but the guards were asleep and the doors unlocked themselves. When he looked down into Devika's arms he saw his son Krishna. Once again he seemed to be an ordinary baby, leaving no memory of Vishnu's visit except the thought that the child should be exchanged for Yashodha's daughter. Accordingly, Vasudev set off for Gokul, the village where his older son, Balaram, was already hidden. He ran until he arrived at the River Yamuna. It was a windy monsoon night and the river, which was several miles wide, roared and thundered menacingly. Desperate to save the life of his baby, Vasudev stepped bravely into the water and walked until the waves covered his mouth and nose. But Krishna reached out and divided the water until Vasudev had completed the crossing.

When he reached Yashodha's home Vasudev secretly exchanged the babies and returned to the palace where the doors were locked again behind him and the guards awoke with no memory of having slept.

Kans was immensely relieved to hear that Devika had given birth to a daughter and immediately released the couple, asking their forgiveness. But as he left the chamber a voice said in his ear, 'Your destroyer has been born.' Wild with fear and rage, Kans ordered the death of all the baby boys in the city. However, Krishna was safe with Yashodha and her husband, Nand, in Gokul.

Krishna and the whirlwind

All of the villagers celebrated when the astrologers forecast that the young boy born to Nand and Yashodha would be a famous slayer of demons, but Krishna's childhood was filled with many dangers. King Kans soon discovered the truth about who was to be his destroyer, but he knew that Krishna would have to be killed by magical means since none of his soldiers would be able to harm the baby.

When Krishna was only six months old, Kans sent a demoness named Putana disguised as a gentle young woman who had lost her children and husband in a famine. The kindly Yashodha employed her as Krishna's nurse but Putana filled her breast with poison and put Krishna's mouth to it. However, the poison had no effect on Krishna. Instead he sucked with such ferocity that he emptied the woman's body of all her energy and soon she lay dead on the floor in her own hideous form.

King Kans was more determined than ever to kill Krishna while he was still a child, and he was constantly searching for demons and other evil creatures who would be cunning and strong enough to do his work for him. One day the demon Trinavarta came to him with an idea. 'I will turn myself into a whirlwind,' he said, 'and carry him off with me. I will smash him against rocks and expose him to the chill snows of the Himalayan peaks and the baking heat of the infernal regions. Then I shall fly him to the highest point in the universe and dash him into the depths of the cosmic ocean.'

Kans chuckled to himself. 'An excellent plan, Trinavarta,' he replied. 'Nothing could survive such treatment. Go, fulfil your mission!'

Trinavarta immediately flew to Gokul and transformed himself into a strong, slow wind which whirled in circles over the ground, whipping up the dust and spreading it over the countryside. As the wind rose and gathered momentum the sky over Gokul was filled with grit and the day became as dark as night. Yashodha ran out of her house hoping to find the baby Krishna who was playing in the yard, and bring him out of the storm into the safety of the house. But she could see nothing in the blackness. She screamed his name repeatedly, but Krishna did not come to her nor did he answer her calls, for the hideous moans and shrieks of the whirlwind were so loud that he could not hear her voice.

Under cover of the darkness, Trinavarta grabbed Krishna and flew with him into the sky, buffetting him among the clouds, pulling him down and flying up with him, but always clenching him in a suffocating grip. As he soared upwards at great speed the demon noticed that the child's body was beginning to grow heavier and heavier until he weighed more than the most enormous mountain. Trinavarta was no longer able to bear Krishna's weight and began to fall earthwards until with a horrific scream he was dashed against the ground and instantly killed.

At once, the sky cleared again, sunlight flooded back into the day and the fearsome noises ended. Yashodha peered anxiously from a window and, calling Krishna's name, caught sight of her son chortling merrily beside the corpse of the mighty demon. She rushed to him immediately and scolding him affectionately for his naughtiness, carried him into the house. Krishna, quite unashamed, winked cheekily at the village girls who had gathered to see what was happening.

In the same way other fiends were sent by Kans but Krishna destroyed them all without coming to any harm, just as he would eventually overthrow King Kans, yet at the same time he continued to be a cheerful baby who endeared himself to everyone around him.

Radha and the gopis

Krishna and his brother Balaram grew up among the goat and cowherds in Gokul. Krishna became well-known for the beauty of his flute-playing and for his sense of mischief which frequently upset the gopis (herd-girls) who spent much of the day milking the cows then churning butter. Krishna had a passion for butter and as soon as he could walk, he would climb the shelves in the dairies in search of

butter and yoghurt. The gopis often complained to Yashodha who spanked him and warned him not to steal again, but Krishna often made her laugh with his impertinent denials. Often the little boy claimed the gopis had offered him the butter: at other times he claimed the butter was payment for some work he had done for them.

Once Yashodha caught her son red-handed sitting in the centre of a group of boys to whom he was handing large lumps of butter, spilling some in the process. When the child saw his mother, he looked up innocently, still holding the butter churn in one hand, his hands and mouth smeared with butter.
'I do not know who spilled the buttermilk or took the butter,' he said. 'I am innocent.'
Unable to stop her laughter, Yashodha nevertheless dragged Krishna away and tied him to a wooden pole in her yard to keep him out of mischief.

While he was there, the gods told Krishna that he had to rescue two men who had been turned into trees by demons and were condemned to stay like that until Krishna released them. With a mighty heave the little child wrenched the wooden pole out of the earth and made his way to two trees in the nearby forest, still carrying the pole on his back. He uprooted the trees which turned into two men who fell to the boy's feet and thanked him again and again for saving them. The gopis and cowherds saw the miracle but still did nor realize who Krishna was—instead they praised the gods for the strength they had given him.

One day while playing in a yard, Krishna swallowed some clay. When Yashodha found out she opened his mouth to have a look and saw the three worlds of Heaven, Earth and Sky in it. She fell silent, and told herself that she was being foolish for thinking that the god Vishnu had made his home with her. When she looked again, Vishnu had disguised himself once again and he made all knowledge of the vision vanish from Yashodha's mind.

The years passed peacefully, and Krishna grew up into a handsome young man, entrancing everyone with the magic of his flute which he used to call back lost cattle and cowherds alike. The milkmaids all fell

hopelessly in love with him and realized that he was blessed by Vishnu.

'If only we could all be flutes,' they thought longingly, 'so that we could be constantly caressed by Krishna's lips.'

He knew their love for him and often teased them. One day as the young girls bathed in the river, Krishna stole their clothes and took them up into a nearby tree. When the girls looked around they saw Krishna in the tree dressed in saffron robes, his head and neck covered with garlands and with the blue skin of Vishnu himself. The girls realized that he was indeed the embodiment of Vishnu and, ashamed of their nakedness, they crouched down into the water. However, Krishna spoke to them gently. 'Clothes matter little in the other life,' he said. 'Your nakedness is merely a sign of your closeness to me. A child is not shamed before its father nor a wife before her husband. So come one by one and take your clothes from me. While you are in this world, you need to cover yourselves with them for this is the world of material things where show and customs matter.'

When they had dressed themselves again, Krishna promised each of the girls that he would dance with them on the night of the full moon and, overjoyed, they all returned home to their husbands.

Of all the gopis, Radha loved Krishna the most and she took great risks to see him. So, after the dance of the full moon had been performed, Krishna took Radha with him and disappeared. Soon she became over-confident, and demanded to be carried on his back because she was tired. Krishna was saddened that she still put personal comfort before the company of a god, and he left her on her own. Radha repented and wept, shining in her grief like radiant moonlight without its life-source, the moon. Finally, the other gopis caught up with her and they all sank to their knees and prayed for Krishna to return. When he did so, he took Radha in his arms and embraced her tenderly while all the other girls gazed longingly at the two of them from behind the trees and bushes of the forest. Krishna knew that they were there and to please them, he created many images of

himself so that each girl thought that she held his hand and danced with him. But the real Krishna held Radha.

After this, Radha took increasingly greater risks to meet Krishna. One night her husband found her stealing out to meet Krishna and chained her to the wall. Radha was so full of grief that she could not meet Krishna that her soul left her body and flew to meet him. Krishna took the soul into his keeping, saying that she had committed the ultimate act of love and that they would never again be separated. Radha's love for Krishna was rewarded, for it is devotion and not high birth or great learning that makes a soul immortal.

Krishna lifts a mountain

Vrindavan was a lush and fertile region where crops grew well. Although Krishna was by birth a prince, he had chosen to grow up among its rural people so that in future everyone would know that God was accessible to all and that the riches of kings and the penances of holy men were no dearer to him than the true devotion of simple folk. Krishna knew that the local tribes worshipped Indra, King of the Heavens, hoping that in return Indra would send rain regularly and would keep away the drought demons. Krishna tried in many ways to convince them that love and knowledge of Vishnu could be their salvation so that they would escape the cycle of rebirth.

'You are people of the soil,' he told them, 'why should you need to worship a king, even if he is King of Heaven? Vishnu is in all things, and no amount of sacrificial offerings to Indra can change what Vishnu has planned. Rather than worshipping a useless god, it would be better to worship the land, Mount Govardhan which shelters you from the elements, and the streams it sends to water your forests and crops. Worship them and you worship Vishnu.'

'But Indra looks after us so well that our land is always heavy with crops that are ready for harvesting,' the people replied. 'We should like to leave things as they are.'

Krishna knew that this was not Indra's doing, but was directly related to Vishnu's function as the preserver of the world, and he continued to persuade the villagers to worship the God revealed in nature. Finally he convinced them, and the people began bringing offerings to Mount Govardhan. In order to give them a clear sign that they had done the right thing, Krishna projected a portion of himself onto the mountain top, appearing to them as the mountain god while Krishna the cowherd remained firmly beside his father Nand. The mountain god accepted their sacrifices and blessed their offerings, but Indra was furious at the loss of his worshippers.

'The only way to bring them back to me,' he fumed, 'is to show them some of my power.' He commanded the rains to pour without stoping on Vrindavan until the people began to think the end of the world had come and that they would surely all be washed away. 'Krishna,' they implored, 'you told us Govardhan would protect us from the elements—do something, tell him to save us.'

Krishna looked directly at the great mountain and directed the energy of his body into its centre until the mountain glowed and sizzled with his heat. Then Krishna grew to an enormous size and, reaching out one of his powerful arms, lifted Govardhan onto his little finger. He brought it into the skies above Vrindavan to shelter the crops from Indra's anger. The rain continued to pour, but as it struck the hot mountainside it hissed and boiled away. For seven days the rain did not cease and for seven days Krishna held the mountain on his little finger without tiring or shifting position. All that time not a drop of rain fell on any part of Vrindavan.

After a week had passed, Indra ended the rains and acknowledged that Krishna was indeed the incarnation of Vishnu, the Supreme Being. Krishna set Govardhan down once again, and Indra arrived to pay Krishna his respects. Mounted on his magnificent elephant Airavati, Indra came to Krishna and bowed before him in front of all Vrindavan, pledging his allegiance. After this, Krishna became known as Giridhar, the mountain wielder.

The Bhagavad Gita—the song of Krishna

Krishna had been brought up as a simple cowherd, but he knew it was his duty to kill King Kans one day. Kans also still wanted to kill Krishna, and eventually invited him to Mathura. He pretended that he wanted Krishna to come to a festival in honour of Shiv—in fact, he intended to ambush him. However, Krishna saw his opportunity to deal with Kans at last, and gladly accepted the invitation.

Kans' first attempt on Krishna's life happened as Krishna and his brother Balaram entered the city. They saw that a huge rogue elephant was chained up at the city gates, stamping his great feet and swinging his vast trunk in fury. Kans' servants released the elephant which bellowed fiercely and charged at Krishna, but Balaram stepped between them and gave the huge animal such a violent blow that the elephant collapsed.

Then Krishna entered the city appearing in many forms at the same time. The festival wrestlers saw him as a wrestler and the clowns as a clown, while to Kans and his demon companions, he appeared as Death itself.

As Krishna entered the arena where the festival was being celebrated, he was challenged by the wrestlers whom he defeated in swift succession. When he had overcome the last of them, he leaped onto the dais where Kans sat and killed him in the presence of the entire city. Then he consoled the dead king's many wives. 'Everyone who ever lives, must die,' he explained. 'Do not grieve for your husband. This world of mortals is simply a procession of lives and deaths. Turn your eyes to the other world and be glad that Kans has been released from the evils of his present life.'

Then for a moment he appeared to them as his true self, beautiful and benign, his eyes full of love, dressed in yellow and seated on a magnificent throne covered in white lotuses.

Krishna returned the kingdom to its rightful monarch, and began to live with Balaram and all his royal relations in Mathura. Some time later, Krishna heard that his other relatives, the Pandavs of Indraprastha, had been unjustly exiled by their cousins the Kauravs, and tried to help them. He went to the Kauravs and attempted to persuade them to return what they had wrongly taken. The Kauravs refused. 'The only way to decide this question honourably,' they said, 'is through war.'

Krishna expressed regret that his peace mission had failed but he left the palace without further argument. As he walked out, Krishna was attacked by some of the Kauravs' soldiers. Immediately he made himself grow a thousand times bigger. His eyes flashed lightning and his laughter was like the most violent roaring of thunder. His attackers were so terrified that they ran into hiding. Then he returned to his cousins the Pandavs accompanied by some Kaurav ambassadors.

'The Kauravs want only war,' he told them regretfully, 'and you each have your allies. Although you will be outnumbered, you have no choice but to fight for what is right. I will make both sides an offer. They may choose me to help them although I will not fight or they may choose my armies of kinsmen, the Vrishnis.'

Without hesitating a moment, Prince Arjun of the Pandavs replied, 'We choose Krishna.' Krishna smiled.

'Are you sure?' he asked. 'I remind you, I will not fight and you are short of men.'

Arjun shook his head. 'I have no doubt in my mind Krishna. I choose you over your men.' 'Then I will be your charioteer,' Krishna said.

The Kaurav ambassadors were delighted with Arjun's choice. Krishna would not be actively fighting against them and the Vrishni armies would be on their side.

Over the following days, both sides made ready for war and finally met for the great battle. The Kauravs outnumbered the Pandavs by more than two to one. However, the Pandavs were led by Arjun and advised by Krishna, who drove Arjun's chariot pulled by four white horses. When Krishna gave Arjun the sign, he raised his trumpet and blew powerfully into it, the signal for the battle to begin. In no time at all the mighty armies of the Kauravs and their allies replied so that the sound of their many trumpets shook the air. Krishna turned around in the chariot to see that Arjun had become pale and was trembling. 'Prince Arjun,' he said gently. 'Why are you so full of hesitation and horror just when the battle is about to begin?'

'Krishna,' Arjun replied, 'I look at the other side and there I see my dear uncles, my beloved teachers and my blood relations. I would not kill them to possess Heaven itself. It makes no sense to kill them for a mere kingdom.'

Krishna paused only a moment before speaking in a soft voice that resonated through Arjun's very being.

'Prince Arjun,' he said. 'This is your hour of trial. It is your destiny to fight this war. You are just a weapon, God is the fighter. No man can kill—birth, childhood, youth and death are passing conditions decided and executed by God. It is your function to fight, brave warrior, and you must do so without hesitation.' Seeing Arjun's doubt, he assumed his divine form. 'Do as I say: I am Vishnu, the Supreme One.'

Arjun looked up and instead of his friend and relative Krishna, he saw a vast figure in whose body was the whole of creation: the past, the present and the future were mirrored in him. Arjun knew that he could only do right in obeying. He bowed before him and the figure laid his hand on Arjun's head saying, 'Fight in the spirit of a worshipper.'

For what seemed like an eternity to him, Arjun lay bowed at Krishna's feet while the god sang his divine song, telling Arjun of the difference between right and wrong, truth and illusion, morality and dishonesty, duty and impiety. This song is now written down in a book known as the *Bhagavad Gita*, and it is one of the most sacred books of Hinduism. When Arjun arose at last, he was enlightened. He cast a quick glance in the direction of his men, poised for attack but anxious at the hesitation of their leader. With a new sense of purpose he raised his bow and took aim.

The war lasted eighteen days during which the dishonest Kauravs were entirely annihilated and many good people died on both sides. Still, Krishna's celestial song reverberated in Arjun's ears and drove him to victory, for the war represented the victory of good over evil. The next chapter explains why the war began.

Stories from the Mahabharat

The *Mahabharat* is the longest of all the epics produced by the great civilizations of the world and contains about 270,000 lines. It was compiled in approximately 500 BC and tells a series of interlocked stories centred around two royal families called the Kauravs and the Pandavs. Both families were descendants of an ancient monarch named King Bharat and the epic's title (*Maha Bharat*) means 'The Great (war of the sons of) Bharat'.

Much of the epic is devoted to tales of war, but there are also many moving romances and thoughtful discussions about Hinduism. The epic's long religious episodes also proclaim the importance of the priesthood in such unusual areas as the teaching of warrior skills and even in kingship. Many romances, myths and moral tales can be traced to the *Mahabharat* as it exists today. The *Bhagavad Gita* (p.89), which is perhaps the main religious book of Hinduism, is a section of the *Mahabharat*.

Between the holy River Ganges and the River Yamuna lay the kingdom of Kurujangal which was once ruled by the young King Shantanu from its capital city of Hastinapur. One day as Shantanu walked by the Ganges, he saw a beautiful woman standing on its bank. She had long flowing hair gleaming with silvery lights and was dressed in misty, blue silk which flowed around her like watery waves. Around her waist was a belt of pearls which shimmered and sparkled like sun-kissed waters when they catch the light. Shantanu was enchanted by the sight of her.

'Beautiful maid,' he said, approaching her. 'I do not know whether you are a celestial nymph or a goddess, but you are certainly too beautiful to be a mortal woman. I implore you to marry me, for I am in love with you.'

The woman glided towards Shantanu, her eyes glowing, her clothes flowing about her like the river.

'I will marry you,' she replied, 'but you must never ask my name or question my actions, however unreasonable they may seem.'

Mutely, Shantanu nodded and the couple were married with much pomp and ceremony. The young queen gave birth to a son each year and to the king's horror and anguish threw each infant into the waters of the Ganges saying, 'This is for your good.'

Shantanu kept his promise and never interfered. However when an eighth son was born and his queen carried him to the banks of the Ganges, cossetting him and cuddling him and smiling into his face saying, 'I will free you too—this is for your good,' Shantanu could not contain himself and holding out his arms, caught the baby as she threw him to the waters. 'How can you drown your own sons like this?' he cried, lamenting the death of the seven others.

The queen looked at Shantanu serenely. 'I will give you this eighth son as a parting gift,' she announced calmly. 'Then I must leave because you have broken your pledge to me.' 'I was at fault,' Shantanu said, 'but now I beg you to tell me who you are.' 'I am Ganga, goddess of the river,' she replied. 'I gave birth to the eight gods who were Indra's attendants: they had to be reincarnated as ordinary mortals as a punishment for attempting to steal the holy cow Surabhi. I threw them into the river to wash away their sins and release them so that they could return to Svarg and Indra.'

Saying these words, Ganga stepped into the river and merging with its ripples, disappeared into its depths.

King Shantanu named the child Bhishma, and his son grew into a strong and just young man highly skilled in the arts of the warrior and with a strong sense of right. Bhishma noticed that his father was often lost in thoughts of his mother and felt that he should find another wife. Shantanu always refused to do so until one day, while hunting in the forest near the spot where he had first seen Ganga, he saw a beautiful young fisherwoman. It was spring, and all the trees and shrubs of the forest were in flower. Birds sang and danced, calling to each other, and bees swarmed over the fragrant blossoms. Yet the fisherwoman had a fragrance all her own which was sweeter than any blossom. Fascinated, Shantanu dismounted from his horse and approached her.

'Who are you, young woman?' he asked, 'and are you married?'
'I am Satyavati,' replied the fisherwoman. 'I am not married but live with my father.'

Delighted that Satyavati was free to marry him, Shantanu took her to his palace in Hastinapur and summoned her father. The fisherman came in a great hurry and prostrated himself on the floor when he heard Shantanu's wishes.

'I beg of you, my lord,' he said, 'do not ask me to give you my daughter. She is just a humble fishergirl. What happiness can she have as your queen? After all you have an heir already and no child of Satyavati can ever become king. I fear that my daughter, unschooled in the ways of kings and courtiers, will fret and pine if her sons are unable to succeed to the throne. I beg you—choose another queen.'

Shantanu bowed his head in sorrow. He knew the fisherman was right but he had no intention of depriving his beloved Bhishma of his right to the throne. Besides, Bhishma had all the qualities required of a perfect ruler. Bhishma looked at Shantanu and his heart was filled with sympathy for him.

'Father,' he said, 'I have no desire to become king. I will gladly step down in favour of Satyavati's sons.'

Shantanu shook his head, 'No, my son,' he was beginning, but the fisherman interrupted him.

'My Lord,' he said, 'even if Prince Bhishma

gives up the throne, his sons may grow up and claim it.'

Shantanu was beginning to lose patience with the fisherman's insolent bargaining but Bhishma spoke up again.

'If that is all that stands in the way of Satyavati becoming my mother,' he announced, 'then I swear, with the Sun, the stars and the moon as my witnesses, that I will neither be king myself nor father children who may one day wish to claim the throne of Kurujangal. Are you satisfied now?'

The moment he completed his words there was an almighty roar of thunder as the heavens acknowledged the young prince's terrible oath. Shantanu tried to persuade the young man to take back what he had said, but Bhishma would not do so.

'Then I bless you with this gift,' stated the king, 'death may never approach you until you choose to die.'

Thanks to the oath of Bhishma, the marriage went ahead with great rejoicing.

The Kauravs and the Pandavs

King Shantanu and Queen Satyavati lived long and happy lives together. By the time of their deaths they had had one son, who died before he became king, and two grandsons. The eldest, Dhritarashtra, was strong and courageous, but was born blind and so was considered unsuitable to be king. Consequently, his regent and uncle, Bhishma of the terrible vow, suggested that the younger grandson Pandu should become king, and Dhritarashtra willingly agreed. Pandu was crowned king of Kurujangal and decided it was time to marry. He heard that a neighbouring king was holding a contest known as a swayamvara for his daughter Kunti to choose a husband, and Pandu decided to compete for her hand.

Princes from many countries had gathered to demonstrate their prowess and artistic skills, but when the swayamvara had ended, Princess Kunti went to Pandu and put a garland of flowers around his neck to show that she had chosen him to be her husband.

The marriage took place immediately and soon Pandu and his bride returned to Kurujangal only to find that their uncle Bhishma had journeyed south. Some days later, he returned with Madri, a beautiful young woman and the sister of the king of Madras, expecting to marry her to Pandu. The embarrassed king discussed the matter with Kunti and since it was customary for kings to have several wives, Kunti said she was quite agreeable to the marriage. Pandu married Madri, and the two young queens lived harmoniously together becoming firm friends.

Some years later, Pandu decided to retire to the forest for a short time to meditate and perform certain religious rites, and it was agreed that Dhritarashtra should take over as temporary king of Kurujangal. So Pandu and his wives went to a remote forest where they passed their time in prayer, hunting and fasting.

One day while Pandu was out hunting, he shot a deer that was partially hidden by some bushes. He approached the deer as it fell and found he had shot a doe. Beside her stood her weeping mate. The buck looked sorrowfully at Pandu and spoke to him.

'Alas,' he said. 'We were newly married, this doe and I, and you have killed her even though she was pregnant. Our love has become fruitless. As retribution, I curse you to die the moment you father a child so that you, too, shall be denied the pleasures of children.'

Sadly, Pandu returned to Madri and Kunti and told them what had happened.

'Return to Kurujangal,' he said. 'I must atone for my sin and will never return to resume my throne. Tell Dhritarashtra that I restore him to his rightful position as the ruler of Kurujangal, and live there in comfort under his protection.'

Kunti and Madri, however, were resolute women and deeply in love with Pandu.

'We have no intention of leaving you,' they replied. 'Whether we are destined to have children or not, we will go where you go.'

So Pandu travelled with Kunti and Madri to a secluded area beyond the Himalayan mountains where the stars rest during the day like a million shimmering flowers.

Meanwhile Dhritarashtra became the king permanently in spite of his blindness, and began to rule with the guidance of his uncle Bhishma. Eventually, Bhishma announced that he had arranged Dhritarashtra's marriage to Princess Gandhari of Gandhara, a kingdom on the banks of the River Indus. Dhritarashtra was doubtful that the accomplished and beautiful princess would agree to marry a blind man, but Bhishma set his mind at rest.

'The princess is so in love with you,' he said, 'she has already left her kingdom to come to you. And she has blindfolded her eyes so that she may have no advantage over you.'

Dhritarashtra could hardly believe that anyone could be so deeply devoted, and met Gandhari full of love and gratitude. Soon after their marriage the new queen became pregnant, but two years later she still had not given birth. Bhishma asked a wise man named Vyas to visit the court and find out what was wrong. Vyas examined the queen and told her that she was carrying a hundred sons and one daughter who would all be born in a single large ball of flesh. He asked Bhishma to send immediately for 101 clean earthenware jars and when Gandhari delivered the ball of flesh, Vyas washed it in cool water, then divided it into 101 pieces. He placed each piece in a jar and sealed it, asking Gandhari to begin opening the jars after two years.

At last the two years ended and Gandhari began to open a jar each day. In the first jar was her son Duryodhan, in the second was her son Duhshasan and so it went on until the very last jar yielded a daughter whom they named Duhshala. These hundred princes firmly established the Kaurav Dynasty for the kingdom of Kurujangal.

Far away beyond the Himalayas, Pandu and his wives fasted and prayed daily to atone for Pandu's crime, and still Pandu was deeply unhappy to think he could never have any children. Kunti could not bear to see her husband so unhappy, and spoke to him. 'My Lord,' she said, 'one day before I was married, I received a great sage with kindness. He was pleased with me and told me a secret incantation. If I repeat it, I can summon whichever god I please to be the father of my child. If you permit me to use it, you can still know the joys of fatherhood.'

Pandu wept with joy when he heard the news and asked Kunti to summon Dharma, god of justice and truth. Since the children of gods are born in a single day, Kunti gave birth to a son named Yudhishtra the very next day.

Then Pandu asked her to call upon Vayu, god of the wind, who arrived astride a red deer. The next morning she bore Bhim, who grew to be a man of terrifying physical prowess.

Finally, she summoned Indra, the king of the gods, who gave her Arjun. Arjun grew to be the most famous of all Pandu's sons, for he was beautiful and noble and highly skilled with weapons, especially the bow.

Seeing that her friend Kunti had borne three heavenly sons in three days, Madri asked if she might also use the incantation. Kunti gladly told her the secret words and Pandu asked his second wife to call upon the Ashwins—bright, beautiful beings who were heavenly physicians and the harbingers of dawn. From them Madri bore the twins Nakul and Sahadev.

The birth of his five heavenly sons gave Pandu's life new meaning. He began to take a new interest in life, teaching his sons all he knew about kingship and the skills of the warrior. One day while bathing in the waters which flowed nearby, he was joined by Madri. Forgetting the deer's curse, he embraced her and she conceived a child: within moments he was dead. Madri was so shaken and grieved by the death of Pandu that she too died at once, from a broken heart.

As the couple lay dead in the waters, entwined in each other's arms, they were seen by some Nagas (serpent gods) who told Kunti and her sons what had happened. When the funeral ceremony had been performed, the Nagas advised Kunti to return with the five sons of Pandu to Kurujangal so that they would receive an upbringing fitting for princes. Kunti agreed, and she and her sons were escorted home by the Nagas. They were received with a loving welcome from Dhritarashtra and Bhishma, and the five Pandavs grew up with their cousins, the hundred Kauravs.

The jealousy of the Kauravs

The blind king treated the five Pandav princes with as much affection as his own hundred sons, and his uncle Bhishma also treated them equally well. As time went on the Pandavs started to become more popular than the Kauravs with the people of Kurujangal. Duryodhan, a Kaurav prince, and his second brother Duhshasan began to feel jealous. Duryodhan felt he was the rightful heir to the throne as he was the eldest, and he began to worry that his father and Bhishma might choose the eldest Pandav, Yudhishtira, as king instead of him, since Yudhishtira was a boy remarkable for his honesty.

Duryodhan was constantly fighting with Bhim, the second of the Pandavs, whom Duryodhan often taunted about his vast appetite and burly physique. Bhim usually came off better because he was an incredibly strong boy, being the son of the wind-god. He was good-natured but sometimes fought unfairly if his fury was aroused. Bhim was not the only Pandav who could do things better than his cousins. Arjun was a remarkably accomplished archer even when young, and the twins Nakul and Sahadev were extremely swift runners.

One day all of the children were playing in the palace gardens when Duryodhan hurled a ball upward with the boast that he was strong enough to throw it from Heaven to Hell. Instead the ball fell into a deep, dry well nearby. As the boys stood staring into the well, puzzling over how to retrieve it, they were approached by a strange Brahmin who mildly scolded them for being unable to perform such a simple task.

'I will show you how easy it can be to get the ball back, if only you know the right techniques.'

The Brahmin then broke off a blade of grass and hurled it down into the well with such force that it pierced the ball. He then plucked another blade of grass and hurled it into the well with such a good aim that it pierced the first one. The Brahmin repeated the action a number of times, piercing each blade of grass with another until finally, the chain of grass reached the brim of the well, and he could lift the ball out effortlessly.

The Brahmin told them he was Dron, a famous warrior, and Bhishma invited him to stay and help educate the princes. Dron quickly noticed that in Arjun he had a star pupil. Apart from running, shooting, wrestling and swordplay, Arjun was an excellent archer, and could even shoot accurately in the dark using his other senses. Arjun became the best warrior among the princes and each of the other Pandavs became known for his own particular virtues. The Kauravs became more and more jealous as time went by, permanently in fear of losing their right to the throne.

One day King Dhritarashtra held an archery contest. Predictably Arjun defeated one contestant after another until he was challenged by an unknown youth who said he was Karna, the son of a charioteer. Confidently Arjun accepted his challenge and the contest began. Everyone was amazed when Karna won, and Duryodhan was so overjoyed that he embraced the young stranger and rewarded him with a minor kingdom in the east. This show of favour to a man who had defeated his own cousin was clear proof of the Kauravs' dislike of their cousins—and Duryodhan tried to persuade his father to send the five brothers into exile. Dhritarashtra, however, was a just man and refused.

'I need no help in choosing a suitable king from among all of you,' he said. 'Do not try and influence me one way or another.'

But Duryodhan and his brothers persisted, until the old king began to be worried about the Pandavs' safety. At last, he summoned the Pandavs to him.

'An important religious festival is to be held in Varanavat,' he said, 'I think you should take your mother with you and go there on a pilgrimage.'

The five young men agreed willingly and set off with their mother. When the Pandavs and Kunti arrived at Varanavat, they found that a magnificent palace had been prepared for them. Excitedly they began to explore it, and very soon discovered that the palace had only recently been constructed and that it contained a great deal of materials that could easily catch fire. The pillars and walls were of scarlet resin, the hangings were made of jute and the flowers which decorated the halls, stairways and corridors were modelled from wax. The Pandavs knew immediately that something was wrong and they knew that their great-uncle was also worried about them when after a few days a man arrived at their door.

'I am a miner sent by your great-uncle Bhishma,' he said. 'I am to dig a large tunnel for you so that you may escape if you need to.'

In the following weeks the brothers thoroughly explored the surrounding countryside and waited to see what would happen. It was not long before their palace was set on fire on the orders of the Kaurav princes, but while the building burned in great flames which leaped to the sky and could be seen for miles, the Pandav princes and Kunti escaped through the tunnel and made their way to a forest where they decided to rest. Meanwhile news of their death was sent to the eager young Kauravs who breathed a sigh of relief, thinking that they no longer needed to fear anything from their cousins.

The exhausted Pandavs slept in the forest while only Bhim stayed awake and kept watch. They did not realize that the forest belonged to the ferocious demon Hidimb-asur and his sister Hidimba. Smelling human flesh, Hidimba went in search of them and found Bhim guarding his four sleeping brothers and his mother. Hidimba immediately fell in love with the young man, and she turned herself into a beautiful woman to approach him. Just then her brother arrived in search of her and seeing she had fallen in love with a mortal, challenged Bhim to a fight. Bhim was so strong that he had no trouble slaying the demon. Hidimba then went to Kunti.

'My brother is dead,' she lamented, 'I now have no protection. I appeal to you as a woman to see my problem and ask Bhim to marry me.'

Kunti consulted Yudishthra, her eldest son, who agreed that the request was reasonable. The marriage took place and Hidimba became an ideal daughter-in-law and a good wife. Shortly after the marriage she became pregnant, and Hidimba sadly explained to Kunti that it

was the custom for humans to leave the forest after a demon's child was born. Hidimba gave birth to a son named Ghatotkach, and like all demons, he was born fully grown and with supernatural powers. The Pandavs now prepared to leave the forest as Hidimba had asked and make their home elsewhere. As Bhim said goodbye to his son, Ghatotkach pledged allegiance to him.

'If you need me at any time father,' he vowed, 'all you have to do is think of me and I will come to your aid.'

After leaving Hidimba's forest, the Pandavs journeyed to the village of Ekchakrapur disguised as Brahmins. Shortly after their arrival they discovered that the village was plagued by a demon who lived in a tunnel on the outskirts. Each day the villagers had to send him a cart full of food drawn by two bullocks. The demon ate everything that was sent to him including the driver of the cart. When the Pandavs heard about this, they decided to rid the villagers of this monster. That night Bhim drove the cart to the demon and when he emerged from his cave to eat his grisly meal, challenged him to combat. Soon the demon was dead and the villagers rejoiced at having been released from his terrifying clutches.

The Pandavs continued to live in exile and rid the world of demons who eventually began to skulk away and refrain from doing anything that might incite the Pandavs' rage.

The marriage of Draupadi

One day, some travellers passed through their village.

'We are from the kingdom of Panchal,' they said. 'King Drupad has decided it is time for his daughter Draupadi to choose a husband. Draupadi is famous for her beauty and wisdom so kings and princes from all over India are coming to compete for her hand.'

The five Pandav princes decided they would attend Draupadi's swayamvara. They asked Kunti's permission to do so and set off for Panchal still disguised as poor Brahmins. There the Pandavs found that among the many powerful kings and princes competing for the hand of the wonderful princess, were their cousins the Kaurav princes Duryodhan and Duhshasan. As they were assessing the competition, a hush fell over the assembly for Princess Draupadi had arrived, led by her brother Dhrishtadyumna who was well known as a splendid warrior.

Draupadi was a tall, willowy woman, with raven-black hair that fell to her feet. She had a dark skin which glowed like polished mahogany and was as fragrant as blue lotuses. Her eyes were as large as a lotus petal and glistened like morning dew. Deep in his heart, Drupad had hoped that Draupadi would marry Arjun whose reputation as an archer had greatly impressed the old king. However, when news of the Pandavs' deaths reached Drupad, he decided to create a competition so difficult that only a man with the skill and strength of Arjun could hope to win it.

Dhrishtadyumna now pointed to an amazingly high tower in the centre of the arena where Draupadi's suitors had gathered.

'At the top of this tower is a ring in which is placed a revolving fish. The man who succeeds in hitting the eye of the fish five times in succession with this bow will win the hand of Draupadi.'

A murmur of consternation went through the assembly. Then the kings and princes began to take turns at hitting the target, but the target was minute and the bow so heavy that hundreds tried and lost before it was finally Arjun's turn.

As Arjun approached the centre of the arena, Draupadi looked at him with interest. 'He is undoubtedly a man of beauty and strength,' she thought to herself, 'but he is simply a poor Brahmin. How could he possibly have the skill to compete against such able warriors?' As she watched, however, she found herself wishing this stranger would win the contest and waited anxiously as Arjun effortlessly raised the mighty bow and taking careful aim shot the eye of the fish five times in succession. Draupadi immediately rose and walked over to him. As she placed the winner's garland around his neck, a riot broke out among the other contestants.

'Are you not ashamed to be defeated by an impoverished Brahmin,' Duryodhan cried and roused the other contestants to attack Arjun. Bhim fought off the attackers while his brothers formed a ring around Draupadi and led her off towards their village. In all the confusion, Arjun and his brothers were unable to meet King Drupad and identify themselves. Drupad was naturally curious and somewhat concerned for the well-being of his daughter. He sent his son Dhrishtadyumna after the Brahmins to find out more about them.

Arjun and his brothers went straight home with Draupadi. When they arrived, Arjun burst into the house exclaiming, 'Mother, look what I have won today!' Kunti was busy cooking and spoke without looking around.

'Whatever it is,' she said, 'I hope you will share it out equally with your brothers.'

Arjun was dumbfounded for a moment, then recovering himself he looked at his brothers and at Draupadi, who had entered the room in time to hear Kunti's words. Now Kunti, too, turned around and saw Draupadi. For a moment she was elated at the knowledge that her son had won Draupadi for his wife, but in a second, her delight changed to dismay, for she realized what she had asked her son to do.

'Oh dear!' she exclaimed. 'What have I said!' Yudhishtra immediately came to the rescue. 'Arjun won Draupadi,' he said, 'He should marry her.'

'Would you have me commit a sin by disobeying my mother's orders?' Arjun argued.

'My son,' Kunti protested, 'I spoke without knowing the significance of my words. You must not take them to heart.'

But Arjun was adamant, Draupadi was confused and distressed, and so the twins Nakul and Sahadev were sent to ask the wise man Vyas about their problem.

When Vyas arrived, he spoke for a few moments to Draupadi. Then he explained to them all why Kunti had said those words. Draupadi had apparently been a highly accomplished woman in a previous life. Her father, however, had been unable to find her a husband in spite of her great knowledge. She had therefore decided to pray to Shiv to ask for a husband. When eventually Shiv appeared to her, she was so embarrassed by her own request that she was unable to speak yet was afraid to anger Shiv by being silent and had forced the words out. 'I want a husband,' she had blurted out, and in her fear and awkwardness she had repeated the sentence five times. Amused, Shiv had decided to play a prank on her.
'In that case,' he had announced merrily, 'you shall have five husbands.'

Devastated by Shiv's words, the girl had pleaded with him to give her just one husband. 'I cannot withdraw my words,' he had smiled, 'but I can defer the pronouncement so that you marry five husbands in another life.'

Vyas explained that Draupadi was simply fulfilling her destiny and that no-one must attempt to argue with fate. So it was that Draupadi's brother arrived in time to see his sister married to the five Pandav princes. Distressed and angry, he returned to Drupad to report what he had found. The king himself came to the village, and discovered why this strange marriage had happened. He gave his blessing with pleasure, realizing that the five Brahmins who had married his daughter were none other than the Pandav princes.

Very soon the news of the Pandavs' escape and marriage reached the Kauravs, and Duryodhan began to fear his cousins' revenge. He and his brothers tried to convince their father and great-uncle Bhishma that they should exile the Pandavs or lead a war against them but failed. Bhishma was adamant that the kingdom

should be divided in half and shared equally with the Pandavs. King Dhritarashtra agreed and at last, word was sent to the Pandavs that they were to return to Kurujangal and claim their half of the kingdom. The Pandavs were greeted with love and affection by their uncle and great-uncle and given the hilly northern half of the kingdom. Without complaint they set about levelling the land and building on it houses, gardens and fountains until it was a city so beautiful that it became known as Indraprastha, after Indra's heaven.

The great war

Since Yudhishthra was the eldest Pandav, he was crowned king of Indraprastha and the five brothers and Draupadi lived in great happiness in their splendid palace. The people of the kingdom also lived in great comfort and the Pandavs gained a widespread reputation for their goodness and their courageous exploits.

The Kauravs became jealous of their cousins' popularity. They and an uncle named Shakuni hatched a plot and challenged Yudhishtra to a game of dice, since it was well-known that this was Yudhishtra's only weakness. After much persuasion, their blind father King Dhritarashtra agreed to the match. Yudhishtra knew that Shakuni was a cunning cheat at dice. However his honour would not permit him to refuse the challenge, and so the Pandavs went to their cousins' palace for the game.

The game began and it was not long before Shakuni began to use sly tricks to cheat Yudishthra. Yudhishtra, however, kept playing, becoming more and more reckless as the game went against him and staking everything that he had. Finally, he wagered his palace, kingdom and everything within it for a period of thirteen years. Of course, he lost and he and his family started to leave. However, before the Pandavs left the palace, Duryodhan insultingly told Draupadi to come and sit in his lap, and his brother Duhshasan taunted her with the words, 'You are our property now, your husband has lost you to us in this dice game.' When Draupadi resisted, Duhshasan grabbed her veil and pulled at it.

Bhim was a guest in his cousins' home and so could not hurt them, but he swore that one day he would break the thigh which Duryodhan had told Draupadi to sit on, and drink Duhshasan's blood for his insults. Finally, with nothing left, Yudhishthra and all his household were forced into exile.

Many years passed and the Pandav brothers lived the lives of wanderers. However, they never forgot their ideals and these helped make them many excellent friends among the kings of lands they travelled through. Many of the kings promised to be the Pandavs' allies should they ever need their help.

Arjun and his family performed many heroic exploits until the period of their exile had ended. When thirteen years had been completed, the Pandav princes approached their allies and held a council where it was decided that the Kauravs must be asked to return Indraprastha to its rightful rulers. The god Krishna even acted as their ambassador, but Duryodhan wanted to fight them and refused to give back anything. Accordingly, both sides prepared for war.

The Kaurav armies far outnumbered those of the five Pandavs and their allies. The Kaurav army was led by Bhishma, who was broken-hearted at fighting his beloved nephews the Pandavs, but he considered it his duty to fight on the side of the crowned head of Kurujangal. Prince Arjun, too, was reluctant to fight his friends and relations, but Krishna explained that it was his duty as a warrior to fight for what is right. When Arjun still hesitated, he appeared to him as the god Vishnu to show that what he said was true. On the first day Bhim fought Bhishma, who wore white armour and rode a silver chariot. Bhishma's silver beard and locks waved in the breeze, and gave him the appearance of a full moon on a clear night. They met in battle but neither was seriously injured.

On the second day, Bhim killed the sons of the Kaurav ally Magadha, and then felled the king's elephant in one blow, killing the king as well. The battle raged furiously for days, and each night the two sides would retire to mourn the loss of their own men and their relatives on the other side.

The Pandavs were particularly heavy-hearted. They had no desire to kill their cousins or childhood friends. Arjun hoped to take his much-loved teacher Dron alive, but his father-in-law Drupad was determined to kill Dron, because it was Dron who had taken part of his kingdom from him many years before. Most especially, the Pandavs did not wish to kill their great-uncle Bhishma. However, they need not have worried. Bhishma had been blessed by his father many years before so that he could decide himself when he would die. Accordingly, since he felt that he had lived long enough, Bhishma chose to die at the hands of Arjun, the noblest and most able of the warriors on the battlefield.

On the tenth day of the battle, Arjun's arrows struck Bhishma who collapsed to the ground. As he fell, he called out for his head to be supported: Arjun immediately shot three arrows into the ground to form a bed and

gently raised Bhishma's head to rest upon them. The great-uncle and nephew then embraced and Bhishma told Arjun that he would stay alive until the end of the war. However command of the Kaurav armies was now handed over to Dron the Brahmin who fought tirelessly until on the fourteenth day Bhim and Drishtadyumna decided to play a trick on him.

Bhim's elephant was named Ashvathamman, the same name as Dron's only son, whom Dron loved above all else. Bhim now killed the elephant and ran towards Dron crying, 'Ashvathamman is dead!'
'I don't believe you—you are trying to trick me,' Dron cried above the clamour of the battle. 'Only when your brother Yudhishtra tells me that my son is dead will I believe it.' It was well known that Yudhishtra was unable to tell a lie.

But Yudhishtra confirmed the statement three times, saying 'The elephant Ashvathamman is dead.' However he whispered the first two words so quietly that Dron did not hear them and handed over command of the army to Karna the archer-king. Then Dron fell into profound meditation and his soul left his body. Drupad's son crept up on Dron without knowing that he was already dead and cut off his head. For one moment, two bright suns appeared in the sky before one disappeared beyond the clouds.

Still the war continued. Bhim's son the demon Ghatotkach had helped with his demon armies since the beginning of the war, using illusions to frighten the Kauravs into retreating on many occasions. Now Ghatotkach faced the archer-king Karna. Ghatotkach created a magic mountain but Karna destroyed it with a thunderbolt given to him by Surya the Sun god. Then Ghatotkach produced a thunder cloud which rained stones, but Karna blew it away with an amulet from the wind-god. Finally Ghatotkach became invisible and showered blazing torches and swords on Karna's men.

Karna's terrified soldiers begged Karna to use a magical weapon that the god Indra had given him. It could kill anyone but could be used once only, and Karna did not wish to waste it. Seeing the frenzy of his men, however, Karna hurled the weapon at Ghatotkach, and it

pierced his heart. Ghatotkach knew the end had come, but he still tried to help his father. He grew to a massive size and set himself on fire before falling blazing onto an entire battalion of Karna's men, killing them all as he himself fell dead. The Pandavs mourned his heroic death, but Krishna consoled them, saying that Ghatotkach's death would be glorified by their imminent victory.

On the seventeenth day, Bhim killed Prince Duhshasan and drank his blood as he had sworn that he would. All the other Kaurav princes had also been slain except for Duryodhan who fled and hid in a lake. At first he refused to leave it, saying that the Pandavs could have all of the kingdom as he himself wished to lead a life of meditation, but Duryodhan was challenged to come out on the eighteenth day and face Bhim in single combat and could not refuse. For a while, Bhim looked as if he was getting the worse of the battle, but then he remembered how Duryodhan had taunted Draupadi after the dice game. Making an unfair move that he had learned in their childhood fights, Bhim aimed a low blow that smashed Duryodhan's thigh and for ever more he was nicknamed 'Unfair Fighter'. Then he dealt Duryodhan a final blow which killed him.

At last the great war was over. The death toll was high and the misery great but the cause of right had won. Yudhishtra now made his way to his great-uncle Bhishma and asked his advice on how to be a good king.
'This is the moment for which I have been staying alive,' replied the wounded Bhishma, and passed onto Yudhishtra all his many decades of experience as a ruler. At the end he asked Yama, the god of death to come and take him away. In this way his father's blessing from so many years before was fulfilled, and Bhishma was finally able to rejoin his seven brothers in Indra's heaven.

From that day on the Pandav princes ruled the kingdom in peace and with wisdom, upholding for ever more the cause of right. Yudhishtra followed his great-uncle's advice and reigned wisely for many years until in his old age he decided to live the life of an ascetic and journeyed to Heaven on foot.

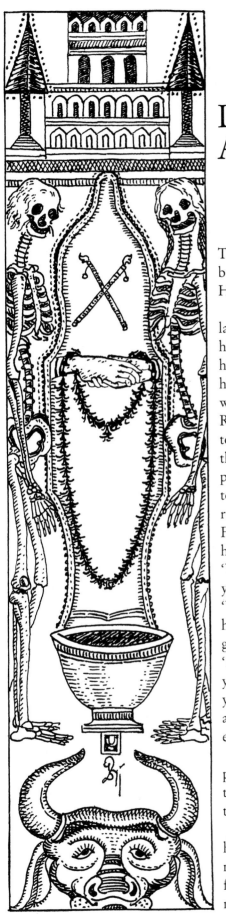

Legends of Romance and Adventure

There are many great tales of romance in Indian folklore: one of the best known is from the Punjab and describes the great love story of Hir and Ranjha.

In the village of Takht-Hazara in the Punjab lived a wealthy landowner named Mauju who was a member of the Jat tribe. Ranjha his youngest son was his favourite, and his brothers were jealous of him, because they considered Ranjha an idle layabout who played his flute while they worked hard tilling and ploughing the fields. So when Mauju died, they divided the land among themselves and gave Ranjha a rocky, barren patch for his share. Ranjha was determined to do his best however and set out early each morning to even out the land and plough it. But it was no use, and finally one day the ploughshare broke on the hard ground. Exhausted, Ranjha sat down to play his flute beneath the shade of a tree and allow himself some rest. Just then his sisters-in-law arrived with the mid-day meal. Finding him lost in the enchanting music of his flute, they assumed he was still an idle good-for-nothing.

'You lazy fellow!' they cried. 'Are you always going to depend on your brothers to feed and clothe you?'

'You never dared speak to me so harshly when my father was alive,' he retorted. 'I want nothing from you or your husbands who have given me the worst bit of my father's land.'

'If we are so loathsome,' the women jeered, 'why don't you seek your fortune somewhere else? Perhaps you should try and win yourself a famous beauty such as Hir. Only someone as aristocratic and beautiful as she is said to be could possibly live up to your expectations!'

Ranjha fell in love with Hir as soon as he heard her name: perhaps they had been lovers in earlier lives and now were destined to be together once again. He silently resolved to do exactly what the women had said.

The very next day, Ranjha left home, taking only his flute with him. He walked for many days, gratefully accepting food from mosques and shelters specially built for poor travellers and when no food was available he lived on dreams of Hir. One night five holy men appeared to him as he lay sleeping in a field. They were all

dressed in white and had long white beards. 'We are hungry, Ranjha,' they said, 'feed us.'

Shamefacedly he told them, 'I have nothing to offer you.'

'Whose is that cow, then?' they asked, pointing to a large brown cow with bulging udders which had suddenly appeared in front of him. Amazed, Ranjha acknowledged she was his. 'But I have no container in which to put the milk,' Ranjha said helplessly. One of them handed him a small begging bowl. Ranjha took it in silence knowing it would scarcely contain two mouthfuls, and began to milk. He milked the cow till her udders were empty, but the bowl did not overflow. The pirs (Muslim saints) drank deeply from it, proclaimed themselves satisfied and handed the bowl, which was still full, back to Ranjha.

'Drink what remains,' they said. 'We know you are hungry too.'

As Ranjha drank, they vanished and Ranjha found himself by the River Chenab which roared and glittered beneath the night skies. Across it was the land of Jhang, his destination.

Ranjha begged a ferryman to help him cross the wide river but he would not agree until Ranjha played on his flute so enchantingly that he did as Ranjha had asked. They dropped anchor on the other side by a beautiful garden filled with fragrant flowers and luscious fruit. Rolling green fields stretched around Ranjha for as far as he could see.

'I am tired,' Ranjha said to the boatman, 'and I see that there is a bed on this boat. Will you let me sleep here?'

'This is Hir's boat,' the horrified boatman exclaimed. 'I may use it to ferry people across the river, but she would have me cut into a hundred pieces if she found a stranger asleep here.' But the strains of Ranjha's flute echoed in his ears and he finally agreed.

Ranjha was awoken at dawn by birdsong followed by the laughter of women and the delicate clinking of glass bangles. Looking up, Ranjha saw what he had dreamed of for so long, because in front of him stood Hir. Her features were like the curves of manuscript written by a skilful scribe; her lips ruby red; her chin like an apple from Kabul. Her teeth were as perfect as pomegranate seeds and as luminous as pearls. Her hair was as black as a cobra sitting on a desert treasure. She was majestic, but her eyes flashed like the weapons of the armies of Punjab on the attack when she saw a strange man in her bed. Ranjha, unable to keep silent, cried out, 'My beloved!'

'Who are you,' she demanded, furiously, 'that you dare to speak to me so intimately?'

'I have nothing to hide from you beautiful Hir,' he replied softly, and told her all about himself and his search for her. He saw Hir's disapproval, but explained that he was sure Hir had been his loved one in many incarnations. Now they had met once more. Then Ranjha played a haunting air which charmed Hir so much that she swore to love him forever.

'You play the flute as well as the god Krishna,' she sighed. 'I could not bear to lose you.'

Ranjha became her father's cowherd and each afternoon Hir would hurry to the river glades where Ranjha looked after the buffaloes. Ranjha would play the flute and they would talk of love. However, this idyll was not to last long for very soon a relation of Hir's named Kaido began to spy on them. He was a well-known troublemaker, and people said that it was because he was lame and could not find a wife that he especially hated young lovers. Very soon he began to gossip about Hir's love for Ranjha until Hir, enraged by his mischief-making, attacked him like a tigress, tearing his clothes to shreds and beating him about the head until he swore to leave her alone. Her actions did not have the effect she intended. Instead of keeping silent, Kaido felt humiliated and wanted revenge—he told Hir's parents everything. They were horrified to hear about the love affair, but Hir begged them to let her marry Ranjha.

'He belongs to a wealthy Jat family from Takht-Hazara,' she explained, 'and only works as a cowherd to be near me.'

'You are the daughter of a Rajput tribe who are famous for their courage in battle,' they shouted at her. 'How can you even consider marriage to a mere Jat? They are only farmers!'

Her family were deeply troubled by the thought that their daughter would dishonour them, and dismissed Ranjha from their service. Hir then angrily went to Kaido's house and, after smashing all his pots and pans, set it on fire. Yet she was not to be separated from Ranjha for long because the buffaloes refused to graze or drink the moment he left, and very soon the villagers insisted that Ranjha should be brought back. Hir's family still disapproved of Ranjha, and they decided to marry Hir to Saida of Rangpur as soon as possible. The marriage had been arranged while the two were only children and Hir did not love him, but the ceremony soon took place nevertheless, and Hir was carried off with the bridegroom's party to Rangpur.

Ranjha was devastated by the loss of Hir, and approached a well-known holy man to take the vows of his order and forsake the world. Hir meanwhile lived in her husband Saida's house but the five saints arrived to tell him that he had no right to treat her as a wife because in God's eyes they were not married. Hir begged the saints to reunite her with Ranjha, and they promised that they would bring him to her. 'But it is the afterlife which truly matters,' they added as they disappeared. Soon afterwards Hir heard that a healer whose flute-playing had a magical quality had come to Rangpur. 'Ranjha has come,' she thought and immediately made plans to meet him. She pretended that she had been bitten by a poisonous snake, and the stranger was summoned to heal her. Hir knew that it was Ranjha as soon as he entered the room, but she stayed as still as she could, as if she was close to death.

'Leave me alone with her,' Ranjha commanded and Saida and his family left the room. As soon as the door closed, Ranjha greeted Hir joyfully, holding her in his arms and explaining what had happened.

'I had forsaken the world and was studying under a holy man when the five saints came to our hermitage. They told me to disguise myself as a healer and go to Rangpur where I would meet you again. Now, my love, let us plan what we should do.'

The following evening Hir crept out of her husband's house and fled with Ranjha. Saida and his kinsmen pursued the lovers, but they reached the court of the king and told him their sad story. When the king had heard everything, he said, 'Your marriage to Saida is void. You can marry Ranjha without any fear of retribution in the court of God or man.'

The couple joyfully celebrated the king's decision and returned to Jhang where Hir was to wait with her family until Ranjha could return with a procession of kinsmen to fetch the bride as was the wedding custom. But Kaido had never forgiven Hir for what she had done to him.

'The king may have declared Hir's marriage invalid but everybody saw her leaving with Saida after the marriage,' he said to Hir's father. 'To sanction her marriage to Ranjha would mean that you condone her immorality and that would disgrace your household.'

Heavy-hearted, Hir's father agreed that Kaido was right and that the only way to guard the honour of his clan was to prevent the marriage by poisoning Hir. Hir continued to prepare for her wedding until one day she was given a glass of cool, lemon sherbet. Moments after drinking it, she fell to the ground calling out with her last breath, 'Ranjha! Ranjha!'

A letter with the news of her death was sent to Ranjha after her burial. As soon as he had read the words, Ranjha heaved a deep sigh and sank back into his chair, dead. Yet the story of the love of Hir and Ranjha is told all over the sub-continent even today and many travellers say they have met Hir and Ranjha roaming joyfully about the river and woodland clearings where they spent their happiest hours in life.

Prince Ahmad rescues Princess Shehernaz

Princess Shehernaz lived alone in the Palace of Wails beside a town on the edge of a magic forest. One day a young prince named Ahmad was out hunting there when he saw her palace. 'Who lives there?' he inquired.

'A mysterious princess,' replied a friend. 'It is said she was kidnapped by a horned giant, and brought to his palace. The giant was killed soon afterwards, but her parents considered her to be dishonoured and did not want her back, so she stayed there. Many brave men have tried to win her hand but she will only marry the man who can fulfil two conditions.'

Intrigued, Prince Ahmad decided to visit the princess. She was the most beautiful women he had ever seen, and he asked what he had to do to win her hand in marriage. Princess Shehernaz replied that every day, just after midnight, the palace echoed with the hideous sounds of wailing.

'The townspeople are terrified and I find the sounds disturbing. Your first task is stop the wailing.'

The young prince visited all the old men of the town asking for clues but they could tell him nothing.

'Many better than you have tried and failed,' replied the old men. 'Many have gone to their deaths. You should give up this quest and return home.'But Prince Ahmad had fallen in love with the beautiful princess and he was determined to have her for his wife. Of one thing he was sure—the cries came from a tormented soul. That night he went to a mound from where the wails seemed to come, and exactly at midnight the prince saw ten ghosts appear from the side of it. Nine of them came and sat beside him but the tenth sat some distance away. Ahmad saw by the light of the stars that their robes were torn and blood-stained. As he watched, plates appeared in the hands of all the ghostly men. The nine ghosts near him talked together for a moment, then handed him a plate, placing some of their rice into it as they filed past. The tenth ghost followed some way behind. As he passed he dropped a rock onto Ahmad's plate.

'The others honour you as their guest,' he groaned, 'I shall do the same.' Then he walked back to his place and sat down again. Ahmad thanked the ghosts for their hospitality.

'I beg you,' he said, 'tell me what this stone means.'

The leader of the ghosts began to tell him their story. About a hundred years ago, there was a village here on the outskirts of the forest in which there lived a gang of robbers. They not only took the goods of passers-by but also killed them mercilessly. One day a large group of travellers arrived.

'Help us across on our way,' they begged the villagers, 'and we shall reward you.'

Ten of the strongest villagers agreed to help the travellers, but the robbers still attacked at midnight, killing everyone and making off with their wealth. Since the ten villagers had willingly died to help others, they were treated as martyrs, but one of the ten called Nuruddin had not been a good man during his lifetime. He was a cruel money-lender who exploited the poverty-stricken villagers by forcing them to pay extremely high interest on small loans. Therefore when the other martyrs magically received food each night, Nuruddin received stones.

'In a moment you will hear him howl with hunger,' the souls of the martyrs said.

'Is there no way of relieving his anguish?' asked Ahmad who was full of pity but the others glumly shook their heads.

'Please let me speak to him,' Ahmad said. The nine martyrs led him to their miserable companion as he sat hopelessly gnawing at the rocks and shrieking with a hundred years of hunger.

'What can I do to help you?' Ahmad asked.

The spirit of Nuruddin looked up at the young prince.

'I never gave a penny in charity during my life,' he confessed. 'I buried all my treasure in the cellar of my house and took more and more from the poor while my gold and silver grew and grew. In fact I had never done anything good in my entire life until I decided to help the travellers. Please help me. If you dig up that buried treasure and distribute it among the poor it would make up in some measure for my earlier sins and I could rest in peace.' As he spoke, the spirits began to fade away and the prince found himself sitting alone on the mound.

Prince Ahmad searched the town and discovered that Nuruddin had no descendants except for a poverty-stricken great-grand-daughter who lived in a tumbledown hovel.

'Bring me news of Queen Mumtaz, wife of Gul Badshah,' Princess Shehernaz commanded, 'and I will marry you.'

Gul Badshah lived in a fortress on a high mountain beyond the magic forest. Prince Ahmad set out on his journey that very day. He passed through the countries of the lions, the monkeys, the birds and the snakes, and eventually arrived at a deep, wide river which encircled the high mountain on which Gul Badshah had his fortress.

It was a dry, hot day and the Sun beat fiercely down on the prince. Ahmad sat down beneath a large shady tree, intending to rest a little before tackling the last part of his long journey. He was just falling asleep when he heard terrified shrieks coming from the top of the tree.

Prince Ahmad craned his neck and saw an enormous nest wedged in its branches. Three huge birds, which were in fact babies of the camel-like bird called the Shutr Murgh, looked down in terror, screaming for help. Ahmad glanced down the tree trunk and saw a poisonous snake slithering up towards their nest. He killed it instantly with his sword. The baby birds thanked him and the prince fell asleep. When the parent birds returned they saw the prince asleep and cried out in alarm.
'At last we have found the enemy. For years he has eaten our babies. We must kill him immediately.'
'Stop!' the baby birds cried, 'this man saved our lives from a snake. Look, its body is over there.'

Gratefully, the adult birds dipped their wings in the cool waters of the river and shaded Prince Ahmad from the harsh Sun as he rested. When he awoke and saw the half-camel, half-ostrich birds standing over him with wings spread apart, Ahmad thought his end had come, but the birds thanked him and asked him what he was doing there. When Ahmad explained he had to get news of Queen Mumtaz the father bird offered to fly him up to the fortress on his powerful wings. As he delivered Ahmad to its entrance, he gave him a feather.
'If you are in trouble, burn the tip of this feather and I shall come to you immediately.'

Ahmad looked around him when the bird

'This is surely not where Nuruddin lived when he was alive,' Ahmad said. The woman replied that his family had inherited nothing on Nuruddin's death. His house had been sold to a merchant whose son lived there now with his family. Ahmad thanked her and promised to be back shortly with good news.

After leaving the woman, Ahmad went straight to the house and asked if he could buy it for twice the price that had been paid. The owner was a good man and he agreed to sell him the house when he heard about the ghost's suffering. Ahmad began digging through the floor of the main room and it was not long before he found Nuruddin's magnificent treasure. He sent for the woman who had helped him and gave her the house and a third of the treasure, buying food and clothes with the rest. Every day for months, he gave alms, food and clothes to the poor and Nuruddin's laments grew softer and softer. Finally, the great treasure was exhausted and Nuruddin at last wailed no more. Then Ahmad presented himself to the princess again.
'I have fulfilled your first condition. What is the next?'

had left. A guard stood in the courtyard.

'I wish to see Gul Badshah,' the prince said, walking up to him.

'Only the hopeless come here,' warned the guard, 'once the king has allowed you to go into the fortress, you may never leave again until you die.'

'I agree to his condition,' replied Ahmad, 'let me see him.'

Gul Badshah repeated the warning but the prince was adamant and so the king made him one of his soldiers. Ahmad searched the fortress thoroughly in the next few days but could not find the queen: finally he was ordered to guard a turret containing an important prisoner whom even the guards were forbidden to look at on pain of death. Each day the prince heard sobbing as a bowlful of scraps were thrown in through the bars of the tiny window, and he decided to peep in. The prince looked down into the dingy, musty room and saw a woman slumped in a corner.

'Who are you?' he asked.

'The unfortunate Queen Mumtaz,' she replied. 'I was put here by my husband after he discovered that I loved a horned giant better than him, even though I was his wife. Now I am locked in here and no-one is allowed to leave the fortress in case the outside world discovers my plight.'

'Which giant was that?' Ahmad asked.

'The one who had a palace on the outskirts of the magic forest,' she replied.

'But that is the Palace of Wails,' Ahmad said, 'and Princess Shehernaz is its owner.'

Queen Mumtaz snarled in hatred. 'The giant fell in love with her and brought her there, but I was not going to let her take my place. I had learned about magic from him, so on one of my visits, I put her to sleep and placed an invisible chain around her wrists and her ankles. I locked it, and when she woke up, she found that she could hardly move. Then my husband discovered where I was. He arrived at the palace with his faithful dog and they killed the giant. After that he imprisoned me here and feeds me on scraps that the dog leaves. However, I have the satisfaction of knowing that Shehernaz is disabled by her chains and can never marry.'

'And where is the key?' demanded Ahmad.

The queen cackled. 'No man can ever reach it,' she gloated. 'It lies in the nest of a family of camel birds in the magic forest. I dropped it as I was being brought here and the mother bird found it and gave it to her nestlings as a toy.'

At last Ahmad knew why Shehernaz had needed to find Queen Mumtaz. He raced to the top of the fortress and thrust the tip of his feather into a lighted torch attached to a wall. Instantly the male Shutr Murgh arrived. Ahmad mounted his back and as they flew away, he asked for the magic key. The Shutr Murgh was delighted to be able to repay the prince for saving the lives of his children and after collecting the key from his nest, he flew him to Shehernaz's palace.

Prince Ahmad presented himself in court for the third time. 'I bring news of Queen Mumtaz,' he told Princess Shehernaz, and told her all of his adventures.

'Hold out your hands,' said Prince Ahmad, showing Shehernaz the magic key, 'and let me free you.' The prince and princess were married that day and lived together in the palace which they renamed the Palace of Joy.

The legend of Sassi

The kingdom of Bhambore lay in Sindh by the mouth of the River Indus and its king was Adam Jam. So wisely did he rule that even the animals and the jinns and fairies who inhabited the deserts and rivers were content to be governed by him. The king's happiness knew no bounds when one day his queen gave birth to a beautiful baby girl, but among the people who gathered in court to bless the child was a fortune-teller who told the king that the child was destined to disgrace his noble house.

Sadly Adam Jam decided that he had no choice but to get rid of his daughter. That night he placed an amulet around her neck and set her adrift on the River Indus in a wooden chest filled with gold coins. Then praying for her safety, he unhappily returned home.

The box floated along the river all night and

at last became entangled in some rushes by the bank. Nearby lived a washerman named Atta who came down to the water each day to do his washing. That morning he arrived as usual and had just begun his work when he caught sight of a handsome, wooden box in the water. He waded in and retrieved it. When he opened the box, Atta saw the tiny baby girl dressed in superbly embroidered silks and wrapped in rich brocade. Atta had no children and so he felt that God had answered his prayers in bringing this baby to him. Hurriedly he took the infant home to his wife and only then did he notice that the box also contained an amulet with writing which he did not know how to read and many gold coins.

'Praise be to God!' he exclaimed. 'Not only has He given us a child but also the means to look after her well.'

They called the child Sassi, and she grew up to be radiantly beautiful. Atta used the gold to educate her and she was filled with a natural grace and charm that set her above all those around her.

One day Atta told Sassi that he had arranged her marriage to a craftsman from a nearby village.

'I have read the story of my birth,' Sassi told Atta gently. 'It is all written in the frame of this amulet around my neck. I think it is time for me to go to Adam Jam and ask for my rights.'

The old couple reluctantly agreed, and Sassi set off to see her royal parents. The king and queen had never stopped loving their missing daughter, and neither had the heart to send her away again when they saw her standing before them. Sassi began to live in comfort in an enormous palace with ladies-in-waiting who became her close friends. One day she decided to visit an art gallery in Bhambore and there she saw the portrait of a handsome young man who had such a soulful expression in his eyes that she fell in love with him at once.

Sassi asked who he was and discovered that

he was Prince Punnu of the desert kingdom of Katch-Makran, and that he seldom left it, because his father could hardly bear to be parted from him. Sassi returned to the palace in a thoughtful mood. In due course merchants from Katch-Makran arrived, and Sassi immediately had them arrested.

'Send word home that only the good offices of Prince Punnu can get you released,' she commanded them.

When Prince Punnu received this message, he set off for Bhambore where he met Sassi and arranged the release of his men. Now this whole episode had been a plan on Sassi's part to bring about a meeting with Punnu and when they saw each other they fell in love at once. Punnu did not return home, but instead married Sassi and stayed with her in Sassi's beautiful palace. However, his doting father was unable to bear the separation any more and sent kinsmen to Bhambore to bring back Punnu by fair means or foul. As soon as they had arrived, they made their way to the palace and insisted on holding a great feast to celebrate the prince's marriage. They drugged the wine at the feast and when everyone else had fallen into a deep stupour, they tied Punnu up, flung him over the back of one of their camels, and raced off into the desert on their way home.

The next morning Sassi awoke to find Punnu gone. She was distraught at the loss of her husband and ran to her father the king.

'Wake the guards and chase after them,' she said to her father, 'and I will come with you as well.'

'We will stay here, and so shall you,' King Adam Jam said severely. 'We are not at war with the kingdom of Khatch-Makran and your husband and his kinsmen are free to leave my country if they so wish. If Prince Punnu truly loves you, then he will eventually come back. As for you, Sassi, the only proper thing for you to do is to wait for Prince Punnu to come back—it would be a shameful thing for a woman to chase after a man even if he is her husband.'

For the next few days, Sassi could not eat, drink or sleep but wandered up and down her gardens waiting for Punnu to return. Finally certain that he would not come back, Sassi left the palace in secret, and ran across the desert to look for Punnu.

Sassi had lived in the lap of luxury all her life even when she was with Atta. She was unused to the relentless desert heat yet wandered determinedly in the blazing afternoon sun. Her slippers were soon torn and her feet were burned by the hot sand. Her lips were parched, her skin baked dry, but she dragged herself ever onward, with her eyes constantly searching for tracks left by Punnu's kinsmen. Sometimes she thought that she saw a pool of water and ran over to wash herself and soothe her burning skin and mouth, but always found that it was just a mirage. Still she stumbled on, hopelessly lost, until she found the hoofprint of a camel. She looked wildly around for more but found none. Poor Sassi was convinced that she had at last found a clue to Punnu's whereabouts: at that moment she looked up to see a traveller staring at her from behind a rock. Sassi gathered all her strength and called to him, but the man thought that she was an evil spirit and ran away, for she looked wild and dishevelled and surely an ordinary woman would not be roaming the desert alone. Sassi returned to the track and falling to the sand breathed her last.

Sassi's love for Punnu was so great that even death could not end it, and her spirit left her body the moment she died and flew to Punnu to tell him what had happened. Although still weak from the effects of the drug he had been given, Punnu managed to escape on a camel and follow the spirit to the place where Sassi had died. When he arrived, he saw that she had been buried by the traveller, who was full of regret at his fatal mistake. Punnu leaped off his camel and fell to his knees, weeping for Sassi and lamenting that he had not seen her before she died.

All at once the sand which covered her began to ripple and undulate until it had moved into dunes on either side of Sassi's body. She was as lovely in death as she had been in life and seemed to be smiling at her beloved husband. Punnu leaped in beside Sassi and the sands closed over the lovers, leaving them protected and alone where no-one could ever separate the prince and princess again.

Stories of wit and trickery

Hindu gods are powerful but not invincible, and even an ordinary person can sometimes overcome them through skill or luck. That is certainly true in the story of King Puranjaya of Ayodhya which comes from the epic poem called the *Ramayan*.

The Danavs were a race of giants who were descended from a great sage named Kashyapa, the grandson of Brahma. He married twelve daughters of Daksha and through them he fathered most of the world's creatures. The Danavs were extremely powerful and enjoyed fighting and harrassing the gods. Once, after a particularly long and hard-fought battle the gods grew weary and called a conference. It was obvious that they would be unable to repel the Danavs without help.

'The most powerful mortal king is Puranjaya of Ayodhya,' said Indra grudgingly. 'He is after all descended from our beloved Surya the god of the Sun. Perhaps we should ask for his help.'

Puranjaya had been given his name (which means 'city conqueror') after he captured the city of another fierce breed of giants called the Daityas. He was known far and wide for his valour and shrewdness in battle. This had often annoyed the gods, who were slightly jealous of him. Seeing this mortal conquer where they failed annoyed them and they often treated him badly, creating difficulties in his life. Now that they needed him, they were reluctant to ask for his help as they were afraid that he would humiliate them by refusing.

'Send Indra, your chief, to Puranjaya,' Vishnu said. 'I shall infuse Puranjaya's body with part of myself to give him strength and through him defeat the Danavs.'

Reluctantly, Indra agreed and went to Puranjaya's court.

'You are required to assist the gods,' he said to Puranjaya abruptly. 'The Danavs are proving a nuisance and we have more important matters to see to. If something is not done immediately, the world will come to a standstill.'

Puranjaya was amused by Indra's haughty way of asking for a favour.

'Of course I shall help, Lord Indra,' he replied respectfully, 'but I have a condition.'

115

'I never doubted that you would,' snapped Indra. 'Of course it is granted. Now hurry. We have no time to waste.'

'Then go on all fours,' commanded Puranjaya. 'For my condition is that I will fight mounted on your back.'

Stunned though he was, Indra had no alternative but to agree. Relenting a little, Puranjaya suggested that Indra disguise himself as a bull to protect his dignity. So Indra allowed Puranjaya to mount his hump from where the king fought and won the battle for the gods.

Savitri: the perfect wife

There was great rejoicing in the kingdom of King Ashvapati when the Princess Savitri's marriage was announced. Her chosen husband-to-be, Satyavan, was handsome and good and lived with his parents in a forest retreat. His father Senapati had once been a king, but his country had been taken over in a court mutiny. Senapati had been blinded in the struggle and had retired to the forest retreat with his family. However, King Ashvapati had agreed to let his daughter marry Satyavan in spite of his poverty, because the couple had loved each other for a long time before

Senapati's misfortunes. Unfortunately, the princess and her parents had a secret grief.

It was customary to consult the astrological birth charts of young couples before their marriage to discover whether the union would be a happy one, so Ashvapati had invited the great sage Narad to read them. Narad looked up unhappily after consulting the charts. 'Satyavan would be a perfect husband, but he is to die exactly a year after his marriage to Savitri,' he told them. Savitri begged her father to keep the matter a secret and went ahead with the marriage in spite of her parents' pleas.

Savitri was a cheerful and devoted wife during the year of her marriage. She prayed and fasted constantly, invoking the protection of her namesake, the goddess Savitri, and begging to be saved from widowhood. Somehow, she knew her prayers had been heard and that the goddess would help her all she could. As the year of her marriage drew to a close, Satyavan often caught a look of concern on his wife's face and asked her the reason for it, but she always gave a plausible explanation. She followed Satyavan everywhere during the last week, waiting for the end. Finally on the last day of the year, Satyavan was chopping wood in the forest when he fell down dead without any warning. Yama, the god of death, stepped forward to claim his soul, but this was what Savitri had been waiting for and she spoke boldly to him.

'Return my husband to me, Lord of Death, or take me with you.'

'Death and Life are not planned according to the whims of a grief-crazed woman,' sneered Yama. 'He must go with me.'

'Then I shall follow wherever you go.'

Yama laughed loudly, knowing that no mortal could leave the boundaries of the world and stay alive. However, the young woman followed Yama, trusting in the support of the goddess Savitri. Yama stopped at the Earth's edge.

'I am about to enter the domain of the Sun,' he warned. 'Only I, Yama, can survive there for Surya the Sun god is my father. Even the other gods cannot bear the intensity of his heat. But as a reward for your determination and strength, I will grant your father-in-law Senapati sight so that he will be able to support you in your widowhood.'

'What good is a father's sight if he cannot see his son?' Savitri replied and continued to follow the god into the kingdom of the Sun, and passed the Sun itself. Astonished, Yama stopped.

'You are protected by some deity, brave one,' he said, softening. 'I will return Senapati's kingdom as a second gift to you.'

'What good is a kingdom without an heir?' Savitri replied and followed the god to the very Gates of the Kingdom of Death. There she caught hold of Yama before he could pass through.

Yama was unable to enter his kingdom with the new soul while the living woman held onto him.

'One last gift,' he thundered, hoping to frighten her away.

'Make me the mother of a hundred sons,' said Savitri.

'So be it!' Yama replied.

'How so, lord?' Savitri asked, 'when I have no husband?'

Yama laughed in admiration at the swiftness of Savitri's mind.

'You are truly named after the goddess of wisdom,' he smiled. 'Return to Earth and find your husband alive. As for the other gifts, you may keep those too, for few people deserve them more than you.'

Savitri returned to Earth where she found her husband alive and well, and her father-in-law able to see. The couple returned to Senapati's kingdom and lived happily together there. And, of course, they had many, many fine children!

Dakshina's wisdom

Dakshina lived in the woods with her husband Ashvin and his father Kanwal Singh who worked as labourers. Dakshina was a cheerful woman although she had not always been poor. Kanwal Singh had been the king of a nearby kingdom until he had offended Lakshmi, goddess of wealth and fortune, by wasting the treasures with which she had blessed him. So she had caused him to gamble away his kingdom. Since then they had lived penniless in the woods of a neighbouring country. Dakshina never complained, because she believed that if she kept her wits about her and remained patient, fortune would smile on her.

One day Dakshina saw a dead snake as she was collecting firewood for the evening meal, and she laid it in the shelter of a tree in the yard to dispose of later. A little later, as Dakshina worked in the yard, she saw a hawk flying overhead holding something in its beak. Remembering the snake, she flung it onto the roof of her house to catch the bird's attention. Then she watched as the hawk dropped the gleaming object and flew off with the snake.

That evening when the men returned, they told Dakshina that the queen had lost her necklace. She had laid it on the window-sill of her dressing-rooms that morning and a bird had flown off with it.

'I have the necklace,' Dakshina said gaily, her eyes dancing. 'I shall take it to the queen.'

Next morning she went to see the queen. 'Is this your necklace, your majesty?' she asked. The queen was delighted. 'What do you wish for a reward?' she asked.

'I wish your kingdom to remain in darkness on the night of the Divali festival. Anyone who wants to light lamps must do so in my yard on the edge of town.' Every year the Divali Festival is celebrated throughout India to bring good fortune, and during it the followers of the goddess Lakshmi light lamps and candles in her honour in their houses. The king and queen did not want to offend Lakshmi by breaking the tradition but they reluctantly agreed to Dakshina's request.

When Divali arrived, the kingdom remained dark but Dakshina's courtyard in the woods was ablaze with light from all the lamps placed there by the townspeople. Shortly after nightfall the goddess Lakshmi entered the kingdom and was appalled to see it in darkness. It was her custom to enter the house of a worshipper for the night and bless it, but without Divali lamps she was unable to distinguish the homes of her

worshippers from those of everybody else. Travelling toward the forest she saw the lights around Dakshina's house. Relieved that her trip had not been in vain, she knocked at the door. Dakshina emerged immediately.

'Go away,' she said, 'you are not welcome here.'

'Do you know who I am?' Lakshmi asked, stunned by her insolence.

'You are Lakshmi and you have condemned us to a life of poverty. You can take nothing more from us.'

Lakshmi did not want to be the laughing-stock of the gods for having been turned away from the door of a mortal.

'Let me in,' she pleaded, 'I will give you enough wealth and good fortune to last for seven generations.'

Hearing her promise, Dakshina relented, for this had been her plan all along. The next morning when Lakshmi departed, she left three golden caskets filled with gems. With these, Kanwal Singh and Ashvin took Dakshina back to their kingdom where they soon regained everything they had lost.

Damayanti's choice

The beauty of Princess Damayanti of Berar was unparalleled. Many men and even gods were in love with her, but she loved a man she had never met—King Nal of Nishadh, because she had heard how handsome he was and how skilled in the crafts of battle and learning. Nal had also heard of her great beauty and accomplishments and loved her too, but neither of them knew of the other's feelings.

One day, while Nal was sitting in his garden dreaming of Damayanti, he saw a flock of swans land in an ornamental lake nearby. Their wings glinted in the sunlight for they were speckled and trimmed with gold, and Nal realized that these were magical birds. Stealthily he crept up on them and caught their leader who threshed wildly trying to escape. When he realized that he could not do so, the swan turned and spoke to Nal.

'If you release me, great king, I promise that I shall do whatever you ask of me.'

'Since you, too, are a king of birds, I believe that you will do as you say,' Nal said. 'Go to Princess Damayanti and tell her of my great love for her.'

The swan flew off, resting only when he found Damayanti in her flower garden surrounded by her handmaidens. Gently he descended and whispered his message to her.

'Tell Nal that I love him too,' Damayanti said, charmed by the beautiful and gentle creature.

Soon afterwards Damayanti's father held a swayamvara to choose a husband for her. Princes came from far and wide to stand in line hoping to be chosen by the beautiful princess, and so did four of the most important gods: Indra the king of the gods, Yama the god of death, Agni the god of fire and Varuna the god of the winds. The princess was so beautiful that even the gods wished to marry her. Knowing that Damayanti was in love with Nal, they each assumed his likeness and stood beside him, hoping to confuse Damayanti so that she would choose one of them as her husband instead of Nal.

Damayanti was introduced to all the men and greeted them with respect, but she passed by each one until she reached Nal and the four gods. She was aware that the gods sometimes played tricks on humans and she had no intention of falling into one of their traps, yet all five of the men in front of her looked identical. Damayanti thought for a while, looking at each one and considering everything about him. Suddenly, Damayanti noticed that the gods did not blink. Nor did they cast shadows. Bowing deeply to the four gods, she paid them homage and offered them her devotion.

'I am humbled by your attention,' she told them, 'and cannot be so bold as to choose a god for my partner. I therefore choose Nal, a mere man.'

Unable to show annoyance because her treatment of them had been so respectful, the four gods admitted that Damayanti had outwitted them and blessed her marriage with Nal, which took place that very day.

Tales of kings and princes

Surya the Sun once sent his son Manu Vaivaswat to people the Earth. The world was soon submerged by a great flood and only Manu survived with the help of the god Vishnu, but later when the world was dry again Manu set about his task. One day he sneezed a son from his nostril and named the boy Ikshvaku.

When he grew up, Ikshvaku founded a great dynasty of kings who ruled the kingdom of Kosala from the famous city of Ayodhya, and many great kings including Ram were descended from him. The *Ramayan* tells many stories about these kings including those about Trishankhu, who was originally called Satyavrat, and Harischandra, yet one of the most famous of all the brave princes of Indian folklore is Prince Hritadhvaj who rescued Princess Madalasa from the underworld.

In ancient times there once lived a holy man named Galav who spent his time alone in prayer and meditation. One day a demon named Patalaketu appeared at his hermitage in the form of a wild animal, disturbing his rituals and making it impossible for Galav to continue his meditation. Patalaketu enjoyed plaguing holy men and so each day he returned to the hermitage as a succession of terrifying animals.

Galav was near to despair when one afternoon a horse appeared from nowhere and he heard a disembodied voice spoke to him. 'This horse will take you anywhere: ride to the court of King Shatrujit on the banks of the Kali-nadi, and ask him to send his son, Prince Hritadhvaj, to help you. Mounted on this horse, the young prince will defeat Patalaketu.'

Galav did as the voice advised and King Shatrujit summoned his son and asked him to help the sage.
'It is an honour that you should be chosen,' he said, 'and we pray that you will accomplish this task and return victorious.'
'I accept the honour laid upon me,' replied Prince Hritadhvaj proudly, 'and will never return to your kingdom until I have destroyed this evil demon.'

The king gave his son Tvashtra—a magnificent thunderbolt that could be used once only—and the prince and the sage returned to the hermitage and waited, Galav sitting crosslegged on the ground, the prince mounted on the magic horse, ready to attack the demon. Suddenly a great white boar came charging out of the scrub towards them.

'That is Patalaketu,' shouted Galav and Hritadhvaj immediately took aim and wounded the boar with an arrow. The boar roared angrily in pain and turned back the way he had come, making for his underworld kingdom, closely followed by the prince. After twisting and turning through the forest, the boar flung himself into a deep, dark pit. Hritadhvaj followed and was astounded to feel himself falling deeper and deeper through a pitch-black tunnel. At last he felt the hooves of his horse land on hard ground and as his eyes gradually became accustomed to the dark, he saw that he was in a magnificent city with golden palaces and high ramparts. But the only light in the city seemed to come from the golden walls of the buildings and the jewels that ornamented them. The city was completely silent and there was no sign of life: no birds, beasts or flowers. Patalaketu had vanished so the prince decided to go back to the hermitage and wait with Galav until the demon returned.

He was just commanding his magic horse to climb the steep walls of the pit when he saw a beautiful young woman entering a splendid palace. Hritadhvaj dismounted and silently followed her through its halls and corridors to a richly decorated bedchamber. On the bed lay another beautiful woman.

'I have good news for you, Madalasa,' cried Kundala, the woman Hritadhvaj had followed, but before she could say any more the woman on the bed had half-risen, seen Hritadhvaj, then fallen back in a faint.

Kundala turned to find out what had alarmed her friend and noticed Hritadhvaj for the first time.

'Who are you? And why are you here?' she asked.

'I am Prince Hritadhvaj,' he replied. 'I wounded a demon who had taken the shape of a wild boar and pursued him into this strange land. But now tell me, who is this beautiful maiden? Have I frightened her?'

'This is Princess Madalasa of the Gandharvs,'

replied Kundala. 'Come, Madalasa, open your eyes and explain how you came here.'

Sadly, Madalasa told her story. The day before she had been waiting in her palace gardens for her friend Kundala to join her, but Palaketu had been hiding there hoping to find himself a wife. When he saw the beautiful Madalasa, he had immediately seized her and carried her off to the underworld.

'As soon as my brother Talaketu arrives with his army, I shall marry you, my princess,' he told her and, unable to contemplate such a fate, she had decided to take her own life.

When Patalaketu left her, she found a sword and was about to kill herself when a strong, sweet voice cried out, 'Do not do it, Madalasa.'

Madalasa put down the sword and looked up. There stood Surabhi, the divine cow who could satisfy all wishes. She gazed at Madalasa with soft, comforting eyes.

'Do not despair,' she said. 'Patalaketu is not destined to marry you. He will be wounded by the one who will be your husband.'

As Surabhi disappeared, Kundala ran into the room. She possessed some small magic powers and had used them find her way to the underworld palace. Madalasa told her everything that had happened and while Madalasa stayed in the bedchamber, Kundala went out to search for the wild boar to see who would wound Patalaketu. When Hritadhvaj saw her for the first time, she had just seen the wounded animal and was so eager to hurry back to tell Madalasa that she had not even noticed the prince.

Hritadhvaj scarcely listened to these explanations: he had fallen in love with Madalasa the moment he had seen her and was concerned only with her.

'But why did you faint, Madalasa?' he asked. 'Did I frighten you? Am I so repulsive to look at?'

Madalasa blushed and did not reply but fortunately Kundala spoke for her.

'I believe that I can answer your question,' she said. 'Madalasa fell in love with you as soon as you entered the room but did not realize that you were the man who had wounded the boar and so were destined to be her husband. She fainted from sheer grief at having fallen in love with the wrong person.'

Without more delay, the prince and princess agreed to be married and, using her magic powers once more, Kundala summoned a priest to perform the ceremony. Although the lovers were now happily married, Prince Hritadhvaj could not return home with his bride until he had fulfilled his promise to kill Patalaketu. They therefore decided to return to Galav's hermitage and await the demon's next appearance.

Meanwhile, Patalaketu had been welcoming his brother Talaketu in another part of the kingdom and had begun to prepare for his own wedding celebrations. As he returned to the palace, he saw the young people disappearing into the upper world and, doubly incensed with Hritadhvaj, who had not only wounded him but also stolen his bride-to-be, he commanded his forces to fight them.

The two brother spirits and their armies soon overtook and surrounded Hritadhvaj and threatened to overwhelm him. Hritadhvaj fought bravely but although he killed many demons he was wounded badly and very close to defeat. Finally, with the last remnants of his strength, he raised his magical thunderbolt and hurled it amongst his enemies. It crashed into them and started a massive fire which quickly burned the evil spirits to death. Only Talaketu remained alive and, defeated, he slunk back to the underworld vowing to avenge his brother's death.

Hritadhvaj had now completed his mission, and he rode back with his bride to his father's kingdom where they were welcomed with joy by the whole population.

Some months later, Hritadhvaj was riding alone and far from home when he met a holy man standing by a river.
'Will you give me your gold necklace, O prince?' asked the sage. 'I need gold for an important sacrifice.'

Hritadhvaj immediately dismounted and handed his necklace to the holy man who thanked him and asked him to stay and look after his hermitage while he was away on pilgrimage.

The prince agreed and with many words of

gratitude the holy man set out on his pilgrimage. The holy man was away for many more days than Hritadhvaj had expected and when he finally returned the prince hurried home, knowing his family would be anxious since he had been gone for longer than usual. When he reached the city, he found it sunk in mourning. The lamps were unlit although it was dark and sounds of wailing and lamentation filled the streets. Even the palace was in darkness. No-one was on guard and an air of desolation shrouded the courtyard. Hritadhvaj jumped from his horse and ran through the palace to his father's personal chambers. The palace, too, was almost empty and the few attendants who saw him stared at him aghast. The king was lying weakly in his bed. He had aged almost beyond recognition and he was weeping uncontrollably. Hritadhvaj ran to his father and held him in his arms.
'Father, what has happened while I have been away?' he asked. King Shatrujit stared at his son in amazement. 'You are alive, Hritadhvaj,' he cried. 'Then the holy man lied about your death!'

He explained that a holy man had come to the court only a few hours after Hritadhvaj had left.
'I am here to tell you that your son is dead,' he told King Shatrujit and his family. 'I tended him as he died and he gave me this gold necklace in gratitude.'

Seeing the prince's necklace, his family had been convinced that the sage was telling the truth.
'I have no use for this,' he said sharply, flinging the necklace at Madalasa. This proof of her husband's death shocked and grieved Madalasa so deeply that she turned pale and fell forward crying, 'Nor have I use for this world if my husband is dead.' The entire court rushed forward to help Madalasa, but she was already dead. This double tragedy had plunged the country in grief. The king had retired to his chambers and prayed miserably for death, but now Hritadhvaj had returned. As the king ended his story, Hritadhvaj said quietly, 'Talaketu has his revenge.'

The holy man had been none other than the

surviving demon who had fulfilled his vow by taking the form of a holy man and causing the death of the one dearest to the prince.

'I cannot bring Madalasa back from the dead, but no-one will ever take her place,' Hritadhvaj vowed.

In the months that followed, Hritadhvaj concealed his sorrow for the loss of his beloved wife and the guilt and shame he felt for having allowed the demon to deceive him. Instead he worked ceaselessly to fill his empty hours and somehow blot out his longing for Madalasa.

One day he was observed by two sons of Ashwatar, the Naga King of Serpents. The Nagas were demi-gods with the faces of men and the tail and expanding neck of the cobra, but instead of one cobra hood, they had three. They could take many forms and often disguised themselves as men. Fascinated by this serious and dedicated prince, they approached Hritadhvaj disguised as Brahmins and told him that they were strangers who had just arrived in the city, and the prince invited them to eat with him at the palace.

The Naga princes were so enchanted by Hritadhvaj that they began to spend all their time with him, and they soon discovered the reason for his grief. Meanwhile Ashwatar had noticed his sons' long absences and was relieved to find that they had spent their time in the company of a prince known for his bravery and virtue.

'What have you given him in return for his kindness?' he asked.

'What can we give to someone who wants nothing but that which even the gods cannot provide?' asked the Naga princes. Intrigued, Ashwatar asked them what they meant.

'He yearns to see his beloved wife just once more,' they replied after relating the prince's sad story. 'Can you help him?'

Ashwatar was moved by Hritadhvaja's suffering and fidelity and promised to do his best. In the days that followed, he fasted and prayed to the god Shiv who finally appeared to him.

'What boon do you seek?' he asked.

'I beg that Princess Madalasa be brought back to life in my palace.'

'So be it, king of snakes,' decreed Shiva. 'She will be brought back to life through your middle hood.'

Ashwatar continued his prayers and fasting and within a few days Madalasa was reborn through his middle hood as Shiv had promised. Ashwatar's wives secretly hid her and Ashwatar then commanded his sons to invite Hritadhvaj to their palace.

'We must go at once,' Hritadhvaj said politely when he heard from the young Brahmins that their father wished to meet him.

'Follow us then,' they said and they left the city and dived into the river.

Prince Hritadhvaj followed them, believing that they lived across the river but to his amazement, they swam deeper and deeper until the surface of the water was far above their heads. To his surprise, the prince found that he could breathe and talk as easily as if he were still on dry land.

When they finally landed on the river bed, the Naga princes appeared to Hritadhvaj in their true form of half-man and half-snake. Hritadhvaj sprang back and swiftly drew his sword, suspecting that he had been lured into another of Talaketu's traps, but the Naga princes reassured him and led him into their

father's magnificent palace. A sumptuous feast was brought in honour of the prince and as they sat talking, Ashwatar said, 'My son, I wish to give you some precious gift which you will not find in the world of men.' As the snake king had expected, Hritadhvaj immediately replied, 'Then give me at least a glimpse of my Madalasa. I yearn for just one last look at her, even if it is merely an illusion.'

Ashwatar arose and slowly drew back a heavily brocaded curtain to reveal the figure of Madalasa smiling gently and holding out her arms to him. The colour drained from Hritadhvaj's face and he stood as if turned to stone. Was this an illusion or a statue, or could it truly be his wife? Hesitantly he moved forward to touch her but Ashwatar stopped him.

'If you touch her, she will disappear,' he warned. 'She is simply an illusion.' Torn by conflicting emotions of joy at seeing his wife again and renewed grief at her death, Hritadhvaj fainted at her feet. Madalasa fell to her knees beside him and weeping with joy at being re-united with him, cradled her husband in her arms until he regained consciousness.

'My lord,' she said when he opened his eyes, 'touch me, I am flesh and blood.' Hritadhvaj

hesitated, fearful that he might lose her if he did so, but Ashwatar intervened again.

'Forgive me, my son,' he murmured, 'I wished to show Madalasa how deep is your love for her. She has been returned to you as flesh and blood by the favour of Shiv.'

Joyfully, the couple embraced and thanked Ashwatar for his great help. They then returned to the city and the prince's parents and lived a happy life together, ruling the kingdom after Shatrujit for many years.

Trishankhu

Prince Satyavrat of Ayodhya was a kind but impulsive man. Whenever he saw something that he wanted, he had to have it at once, and no-one must stand in his way. One day, he saw a beautiful woman in the city and wanted to marry her. When he discovered she was already married, he abducted her. Satyavrat's father was enraged by his disgraceful conduct and on the advice of the court sage Vasishta exiled him for twelve years.

Satyavrat lived in the forest on nuts, fruits and the animals he hunted. Soon after arriving in the forest he discovered that a holy man named Vishvamitra lived nearby but had gone on a long pilgrimage and left his family behind. Now they were poverty-stricken and starving. Satyavrat felt sorry for them, and left food on their doorstep every day for nearly twelve years. Then the land was hit by a severe drought and even Satyavrat could find nothing to eat. One day as he hungrily searched for food he saw a cow nearby.

'That is Surabhi,' he thought. 'If I kill her I could eat for many days.'

Now cows are holy and their slaughter is forbidden. Besides, Surabhi had supernatural qualities and belonged to the court sage Vasishta who loved her dearly. Many decades earlier, Vishvamitra the holy man had tried to take Surabhi by force but had failed. He had remained a fierce rival of Vasishta ever since. However, Satyavrata could think only of his hunger and he killed the divine cow. He was

just finishing his meal when Vasishta arrived.

The holy man was grief-stricken by Surabhi's death and cursed Satyavrat.

'You will henceforth be known as Trishankhu, which means he of the three sins,' he declared. 'You abducted the wife of another man: you killed a cow: you ate its flesh.'

When the twelve years had passed, Trishankhu (as he was now known) returned to Ayodhya and became king soon afterwards. Vasishta continued to advise him whenever a difficult problem arose. One day King Trishankhu asked Vasishta, 'How can I get to Svarg (Heaven)?'

'If you do good deeds and honour the gods,' Vasishta replied, 'then you will go there when you die.'

'When I die!' thundered Trishankhu. 'But I want to go to Svarg with my body intact. Prepare a magnificent sacrifice to propitiate the gods and get them to grant me my desire.'

'It is forbidden for the living to enter Svarg,' Vasishta said. 'I have no intention of bringing their anger on myself by attempting to fulfil your impious wish.'

'If that is so,' shouted the king, 'I will ask Vishvamitra for help.'

Vasishta's old rival was grateful to Trishankhu for having kept his family well-fed during his long absence, and so he agreed to fulfil the king's wishes. He carried out a splendid ceremony by lighting an enormous holy fire and preparing sacrifices. Days passed but no gods appeared at the sacrificial fires.

'Do not concern yourself,' Vishvamitra told the king. 'If the gods do not wish to help me, I shall use my own powers.'

He began to chant a spell, nudging Trishankhu as he ended. When he felt the holy man's push, Trishankhu rose into the air and floated up to the gates of Svarg. Since Indra and the other gods had no intention of letting him in, Trishankhu was immediately given another push and began to fall headlong towards Earth again. However, Vishvamitra raised his hand and commanded him to stop in mid-air. Like the king, Vishvamitra also easily lost his temper and now he was furious: not only had the gods refused to attend his sacrifice but now they were undoing his work. This made him even more determined to keep his promise to the king.

'I will create a new heaven around Trishankhu,' he vowed, 'and fill it with new gods. Indra and the others will be forbidden to enter.'

The gods were distressed by Vishvamitra's threat because they knew he was powerful enough to make it come true, and they feared a rival set of gods.

'If we allow Trishankhu to remain in the sky as a minor god,' they offered, 'will you promise not to make this new heaven?'

Vishvamitra agreed and created instead a constellation of stars to be Trishankhu's companions and there they glitter in the western sky to this day.

King Harishchandra's debt

King Harishchandra of Ayodhya was greatly loved by his subjects because he always honoured his promises and protected those in need, but his personal life seemed dogged by misfortune. One day he was out hunting when he heard cries of distress. Dismounting from his horse, he followed the voices and came to a clearing in the forest where the wise man Vishvamitra was about to conquer the goddesses of the sciences, the daughters of Sarasvati the goddess of learning.

Harishchandra's arrival disturbed Vishvamitra's meditation and the goddesses escaped. Vishvamitra's rage was terrifyingly great.

'You will pay for this, you wretch,' he cursed. 'For years I have starved and meditated to gain control of the sciences and you have wasted all my penances by your interference. Are you honourable enough to compensate me?'

'Ask me for anything,' the king replied humbly, 'even my life.'

'I have no use for your life,' Vishvamitra snarled, 'but I will certainly be pleased to have everything else you possess.'

Harishchandra agreed without hesitation and gave him all of his kingdom. The next day he left his palace with his wife Shaiva and son Rohit to live a life of devotion in the city of Varanasi, but Vishvamitra was waiting for them at the city gate.

'It is traditional to give some money to Brahmins when you give them any other gift,' he said. 'Where is my money?'

'I have nothing left to give,' Harishchandra apologized humbly. 'All that I had is left in the palace.'

'You are well aware that gifts to holy men are accompanied by money. Sell your wife and son if necessary. Unless you pay me 50,000 gold pieces by tomorrow night, all Ayodhya will know that you do not keep your word.'

So Shaiva and Rohit were sold to a Brahmin who promised to treat them kindly, but they fetched only half the sum demanded by Vishvamitra so Harishchandra sold himself to a keeper of cremation grounds for the remainder of the sum. Now that Vishvamitra's demands had been met, the hapless king resigned himself to the knowledge that his life would be spent burning corpses. In a few months, he found that death no longer affected him. He felt quite numb and carried out his orders without emotion.

One night, long past midnight, a woman came to the cremation grounds carrying a small body covered in a shabby but clean shroud. She wept inconsolably but Harishchandra did not try to comfort her. He simply asked for the cremation fee.

'I have no money,' the woman said in despair.

'Then give me your child's shroud for my master,' Harishchandra said.

Startled by his harshness, the woman looked up, allowing her veil to drop from her face. In the light of the moon, Harishchandra saw that the woman was his wife.

'Shaiva!' he lamented. 'What has happened to you ... and to our son?'

'The Brahmin's wife treated us cruelly and Rohit played far away from home to keep out of her way. Today when he did not return at sunset, I went to look for him and found him dead from a snakebite. So I have brought him here to lay him to his final rest.'

Harishchandra looked at his dead son's ashen countenance, at his wife's tattered clothes and his own lowly state. At once, all his human feelings returned.

'We have nothing to live for now that Rohit is dead. Let us burn ourselves on his funeral pyre,' he said and Shaiva agreed.

When the funeral pyre was alight, Harishchandra begged forgiveness from the god Brahma for deserting his master without permission and entering the flames with Shaiva and Rohit, began to pray aloud to Brahma. Suddenly they saw the gods before them in all their glory.

'You have suffered enough Harishchandra,' the god Indra said. 'Come to Svarg and live there in peace with your family.'

'First I must seek my master's permission,' Harishchandra said. As he spoke, his master appeared and was immediately transformed into Dharma, god of justice.

'I disguised myself in order to help you pay your debt, Harishchandra,' he explained. 'I now release you from bondage.'

'But what will happen to my faithful subjects?' Harishchandra asked. 'I could leave them when I became poor but I cannot desert them in my glory.'

The gods then allowed all the king's faithful subjects to accompany him and his wife and son to Svarg, but even now his troubles were not at an end. A minor god named Narad decided to test this saintly king. He praised him lavishly day and night in an attempt to make him boastful.

'You are the first human to have entered Heaven while still alive. You must be at least as wonderful as the lesser gods.'

His words began to affect Harishchandra.

'I have always been better than ordinary mortals,' he said arrogantly one day, 'and I have passed all the tests the gods gave me.'

Indra was annoyed by this change in Harishchandra's character and expelled him and his people from Svarg, but Narad intervened to explain his part in the king's behaviour and Harishchandra humbly begged forgiveness. Indra relented and stopped Harishchandra's descent, creating for him his own city of clouds which can sometimes still be seen today.

Symbols in the Indian myths and legends

At the beginning of each chapter the artist has illustrated some of the objects and symbols that appear in the stories, and these are listed below together with brief captions to the paintings.

TITLE PAGE Prince Arjun the great archer protects a city from demons while Krishna his charioteer blows in triumph on his conch shell. Below, a holy man meditates beside a sacrificial fire. Right, many religions exist in India and are represented by these pilgrims.

p.11 THE WORLD OF THE ANCIENT INDIANS Top, the three most important elements for early Indians—sun, rain and fire which were worshipped as Surya, Indra and Agni respectively. Below them are three later gods of Hinduism: the many-headed Brahma the creator, Vishnu the preserver holding his discus and Shiv the destroyer wearing the crescent moon in his hair. Next come the creators of two later religions: Vardhamana who founded Jainism on the left and the Buddha on the right. Finally there are representatives of the four main categories in the caste system: the Brahmins, who perform religious sacrifices; the Kshatriyas, who are warriors; the Vaishyas, who are farmers and traders; and the Sudras, who are servants.

p.14 THE OLD GODS Top, Surya the Sun god rides in his chariot drawn by seven horses. Next is Indra, who controls the atmosphere and the rain; Vritra the drought god lies at his feet. Fourth is Agni god of fire who rides upon a ram, and beneath them all is Yama god of death, who rules the underworld and rides upon a buffalo. A mace is in his left hand while in the right is a noose with which he catches his victims.

pp.18—19 Agni pays homage to Vishnu and Prince Arjun for allowing him to devour the Khandav forest, and they both raise a hand to bless him. Beside Agni is the ram upon which he rides and in the background is the chariot that brough Vishnu's weapon, his discus.

pp.22—23 Yama, god of death, deciding the fate of newly dead souls. He is holding a mace and a noose with which he ensnares his victims. Behind him is the buffalo on which he rides when he visits Earth; in the foreground his councillor is reading out the life stories of the dead from his register made from bark and palm leaves. Yama's messengers, the Yama-dutas, stand ready to do his bidding as do his monstrous dogs. In the background, Vijaya steps through a gateway of flame into Hell itself.

p.26 THE GREAT GODDESSES Top and bottom, Durga the warrior goddess who once defeated an army of giants and Kali who lapped up their blood. Next to them are Lakshmi who was bathed by heavenly elephants when she emerged from the celestial ocean and Sarasvati who is sitting on a lotus and playing the vina—the swans pull her carriage. Centre left, Sati throws herself into a sacrificial fire to be reborn as Parvati (centre right), who dressed in rags until reunited with Shiv.

pp.30—31 Sarasvati descends from her carriage to find that Brahma has married a mortal named Gayatri. The goddess is carrying the musical instrument that she invented (the vina) as well as a book of palm leaves to symbolize the fact that she is the goddess of learning. Sarasvati's carriage is drawn by a swan and it also contains three other goddesses (right to left) Lakshmi, Parvati and Indrani whose hus-

bands: Vishnu, Shiv and Indra respectively are shown seated directly above their wives.

p.33 HOLY MEN OF INDIA Top, a Buddhist temple and bottom, an Islamic mosque. A Hindu holy man (left) and a Muslim holy man (right) walk together in harmony. Below are the bags that they carry which contain their holy scriptures. Above are medieval and modern Sikh religious books— the former consists of palm leaves sewn together.

pp.34—35 Vardhamana quietens the rogue elephant while his friends run home to Kundigram.

pp42—43 The sultan of Lanka pays homage to Guru Nanak, who raises his right hand in the traditional gesture of blessing. He and his two disciples wear the distinctive robes of holy men and beside him is the basket in which he carries his religious texts. The horse upon which the Guru declined to ride may be seen on the left.

p.47 SHIV, GOD OF DESTRUCTION The god performs his celestial dance while standing on the dwarf demon he conquered. He holds in his four hands a tiger skin, a deer, the demon's club and a drum. Above is the crescent moon which he wears in his hair. Next to him is his faithful companion, Nandhi the white bull: the snake shows that he is also Lord of Serpents.

pp.50—51 Shiv revives Daksha through the power of his third eye, but also gives him a goat's head as a punishment for his behaviour. The snakes coiled around his arms and legs signify that he is Lord of Serpents, and the drum is a sign that he is the patron of ascetics. He wears in his hair the crescent moon which he obtained when the cosmic ocean was churned and the skin of the tiger which attacked him is worn around his waist. On the right are Brahma of the many heads and Vishnu. On the left are the army of demons which Shiv created.

pp.54—55 Ganesh the elephant-headed god battles with Parasu-Ram to prevent him from disturbing Shiv who is sleeping in the background with Nandhi the bull by his side. Ganesh holds a snake to show that he is Shiv's son and is being aided by the magic rat on which he rides. Parasu-Ram is swinging the axe (parasu) after which he is named.

p.57 THE MANY FORMS OF VISHNU Here are shown the first five incarnations of the god Vishnu. Bottom left and right, Matsya the fish and the tortoise with Vishnu also standing behind each: the wild boar which saved the Earth: the lion-headed man steps out of a pillar to tear Hiranyakashipu the demon to shreds: Vaman the dwarf who tricked Bali. Above them all is Vishnu in his full glory holding a conch shell, his club and two lotus blossoms.

pp.58—59 Vishnu prepares to sleep again on the cosmic ocean, lying on the snake Vasuki whose seven heads act as a canopy for him. Vishnu is holding a mace, discus, sea shell and lotus; his wife the goddess Lakshmi (left) and Sarasvati (right) prepare his bed. Some of Vishnu's worshippers believe that he was responsible even for the creation of Brahma who is here shown attached to Vishnu. The flowers which float in the cosmic ocean are lotuses.

p.63 THE ADVENTURES OF RAM Hanuman the monkey brandishes a shield on which can be seen Ram, Sita and Bharat. Above him is Valmiki, the holy man who wrote the epic; beneath him is Ravan, the demon with ten heads.

pp.66—67 The conclusion of Sita's swayamvara in which she is brought to the suitor whom she has chosen (Ram).

A swayamvara was a contest in which many suitors competed to win the bride. Ram (centre) is blue in complexion as are all avatars of Vishnu. At his feet lie the shattered remains of Shiv's bow while behind him stands Vishvamitra who is blessing the couple. The holy man carries a kettle filled with holy water which was more impotant to a wandering pilgrim than food. Sita is carrying the marriage garland in her hand. On the right are Bharat and the defeated contestants.

pp.74—75 Ram comforts Jatayu the vulture while Bharat brings water. The marks on the brothers' shoulders indicate that they are Brahmins.

p.81 THE LIFE OF KRISHNA Krishna plays his flute in the woods of Gokul. Above are some of the cows he tended there. Below, Yashodha sees the three worlds of the Hindu universe in her baby son's mouth.

pp.82—83 Vasudev carries the baby Krishna across the River Yamuna. Unknown to him, he is accompanied by Vasuki, the king of snakes, who is a companion to Vishnu in all his incarnations.

pp.86—87 Krishna embraces Radha while all the other herd-girls look on. He is blue in complexion as are all incarnations of the god Vishnu. He was a famous flautist, and his flute can be seen lying on the ground

p.91 STORIES FROM THE MAHABHARAT Top to bottom, first Shakuni the trickster casts the Indian dice which he used to cheat the Pandavs. These resemble small rods and are played on a tasselled board. Duryodhan pulls Draupadi's veil off her, but she is protected from harm by Vishnu (inset). Krishna blesses Prince Arjun before the battle. A scene from the battle.

pp.94—95 The blind king Dhritarashta sits next to Queen Gandhari, who blindfolded herself so that she would have

no advantage over him. Pandu, Kunti and Madri can be seen walking away into the mountains in the distance.

pp102—103 The great battle between the Pandavs (left) and the Kauravs (right). Prince Arjun fires arrows from his chariot while Krishna acts as his charioteer. Ghatotkach the demon fells a battle elephant with one blow from his mace.

p.105 LEGENDS OF ROMANCE AND ADVENTURE Two garlanded hands are joined together in the Hindu marriage ceremony. On either side are the skeletons of Punnu and Sassi whose love endured beyond death itself. Top, the Palace of Wails. Bottom, the poisoned glass from which Hir drank, and one of the buffaloes that Ranjha tended.

pp106—107 Ranjha plays his flute by the banks of the River Chenab while Hir, the farmers and even the cattle stop to listen.

p.115 STORIES OF WIT AND TRICKERY Centre, a typical Divali lamp that is used to attract the goddess Lakshmi. Below it are two of the magic swans which were messengers for Nal and Damayanti.

pp.118—119 Dakshina kneels in homage to the goddess Lakshmi, who blesses her after staying in her house during the festival of Divali. In the garden are the extinguished Divali lamps and the caskets of treasure.

p.121 TALES OF KINGS AND PRINCES King Harischandra offers his kingdom to Vishvamitra the holy man. Top, an Indian crown from which hang the scales of justice to show that every king must uphold the law. Bottom, the palace which Prince Hritadhvaj entered after wounding the demon.

pp.126—127 Vasishta and his disciples tend their sacrificial fire to enable King Trishankhu to enter heaven. The marks on their arms show that they are Brahmins.

Index

132